Herbert Puchta & Jeff Stranks
G. Gerngross C. Holzmann P. Lewis-Jones

American MORE! 3B

COMBO Student's Book

NOTE FOR TEACHERS

The pages of this Combo edition are numbered in the usual way in sequence throughout. Where the numbers are different from the original full edition Student's Book and Workbook pages, a second number is shown that looks like this: 23. This is so that the page references in full edition teacher components such as the Teacher's Resource Book can be followed easily.

HELBLING LANGUAGES
CAMBRIDGE UNIVERSITY PRESS
editora ática

editora ática

Diretora-Geral Editoras Ática e Scipione
Vera Balhestero
Gerente Editorial e de Conteúdos Didáticos
Teresa Porto
Coordenador Editorial de Línguas Estrangeiras
Luiz Tonolli
Gerente de Qualidade e Suporte
Beatriz Mendes

Assistente Editorial: Danuza Dias Gonçalves
Gerente de Revisão: Hélia de Jesus Gonsaga
Equipe de Revisão: Célia da Silva Carvalho e Gloria Cunha
Edição de Arte: Erik Taketa e Mauro Fernandes
Editoração Eletrônica: A+ Comunicação

American MORE! Combo 3B with CD-ROM/Audio CD
Hebert Puchta & Jeff Stranks
G. Gerngross, C. Holzmann, P. Lewis-Jones

Direitos desta edição cedidos à Editora Ática S.A.
Av. Otaviano Alves de Lima, 4400
Freguesia do Ó – CEP 02909-900 – São Paulo – SP
Tel.: 4003-3061
www.atica.com.br / editora@atica.com.br

Dados Internacionais de Catalogação na Publicação (CIP)
(Câmara Brasileira do Livro, SP, Brasil)

American more! : Combo : student's book / Herbert Puchta...[et al.]. -- 1. ed. -- São Paulo : Ática, 2011.
Outros autores: Jeff Stranks, Gunther Gerngross, Christian Holzmann, Peter Lewis-Jones
Obra em 8 v.
Bibliografia.

1. Inglês (Ensino fundamental) I. Puchta, Herbert. II. Stranks, Jeff. III. Gerngross, Gunther. IV. Holzmann, Christian. V. Lewis-Jones, Peter.

11-13335 CDD-372.652

Índice para catálogo sistemático:
1. Inglês : Ensino Fundamental 372.652

2012
ISBN 978 85 08 15451 7 – American MORE! Combo 3B with CD-ROM and Audio CD
ISBN 978 85 08 14806 6 – American MORE! 3 Teacher's Book

Cód. da obra CL 738263

EDITORA AFILIADA

1ª edição
2ª impressão

Impressão e acabamento: Corprint Gráfica e Editora Ltda.

Uma Publicação Abril EDUCAÇÃO

MISTO
Papel produzido a partir de fontes responsáveis
FSC® C102676

The authors would like to thank those people who have made significant contributions towards the final form of American MORE!:

Oonagh Wade and Rosamund Cantalamessa for their expertise in working on the manuscripts, their useful suggestions for improvement, and the support we got from them.

Lucia Astuti and Markus Spielmann, Helbling Languages, Ron Ragsdale and James Dingle, Cambridge University Press, for their dedication to the project and innovative publishing vision.

Our designers, Amanda Hockin, Greg Sweetnam, Quantico, Craig Cornell, and Niels Gyde for their imaginative layouts and stimulating creativity. Also, our artwork assistants, Francesca Gironi and Elisa Pasqualini, for their dedicated work.

The publishers would like to thank the following illustrators: Roberto Battestini; Moreno Chiacchiera; Michele Farella; Pierluigi Longo; Gastone Mencherini; Giovanni Rolandi; Lorenzo Sabbatini; Lucilla Stellato.

The publishers would like to thank the following for their kind permission to reproduce the following photographs and other copyright material:

Student's Book
Alamy p65, p66 (indie), p69 (Beatles album cover), p70, p72 (bouzouki; tin whistle), p109, p113 (turbine; bike rider), p123; **Associated Press** p109 (Al Gore); **Corbis** p66 (R&B), p69, p74 (US Air Force relief efforts; earthquake damage), p111, p123 (Red Hot Chilli Peppers); **Dreamstime** p66, p70 (boy), p71, p74 (tsunami), p76 (tsunami), p83, p102, p114, p119 (Universal Studios); **Getty Images** p109 (Erin Brockovich); **Günter Gerngross** p99; **Helbling Languages** p86 (modem; notebook; printer; USB stick); **Herbert Puchta** p113 (petrol station); **©iStockphoto.com** p70 (girl), p71 (Steve), p76 (earthquake; avalanche; flood; drought), p86 (DVD-R/W; speakers; flat screen), p94, p95 (beach; camping; surfing), p102 (graffiti removers, girl weeding), p113 (solar cells on roof), p120; **Photos.com** p95 (Statue of Liberty), p115 (Vancouver); **Shutterstock** p66 (rap; opera; jazz; country; rock; classical), p72, p74, p76, p82, p86, p93, p95, p102 (snowboarder), p110, p111 (Barack Obama), p113, p114 (Joshua tree; Walk of Fame), p115, p119, p122; **SuperStock** p102 (teens at construction site).

The publishers would like to thank the following for their assistance with commissioned photographs: Ed-Imaging pp 64, 84, 104, 114.

Workbook
Associated Press p39 (Britney Spears; Buddy Guy; Bob Dylan); **Dreamstime** p39, p44, p46, p55, p56, p68 (Hispanic family; Death Valley; Napa Valley), p72 (American football), p73; **Günter Gerngross** p61; **©iStockphoto.com** p68 (Beverly Hills; gold washing in California), p71, p72 (Joshua trees; black bear); **Shutterstock** p39 (orchestra), p42, p43, p49, p68, p72; **Wikimedia Commons** p67, p68 (The Beach Boys).

Page numbers refer to the original version.

	Grammar	Language Focus and Vocabulary	Skills	MORE!
UNIT 7 I didn't use to like them	• *used to* • *so do I / neither do I*	• music	• talk about what you used to do • agree and disagree • read and match texts and photos • listen to a TV show • speak about performers in a show • write a summary about a pop star or band	Learn **MORE** through English **Musical instruments** **Music**
UNIT 8 Natural disasters	• *too / not … enough* • past passive	• catastrophes **Sounds right** "r" sound	• express sympathy • explain things in simpler words • talk about when people were born • read and understand a story • listen to the story of an earthquake • speak about things to take to a desert island • write about someone who survived an earthquake	**Check your progress** Units 7 and 8 Learn **MORE** about culture **Manga!** Read **MORE** for pleasure **How to survive earthquakes**
UNIT 9 If I had the money …	• second conditional • *If I were you …* • indefinite pronouns *everyone, someone, no one, anyone*	• computers	• give advice • talk about people • talk about what you would do • ask about how long • read about dilemmas • listen to teenagers talking about dilemmas • complete a questionnaire • write a questionnaire **A Song 4 U** *If I were you*	Learn **MORE** through English **Number challenges** **Math**
UNIT 10 Into the wilderness	• make deductions • causative *have* • infinitives of purpose	• vacations **Sounds right** Question intonation	• give reasons • talk about vacation plans • make deductions • read emails about a trip • listen to an email • write a summary	**Check your progress** Units 9 and 10 Learn **MORE** about culture **Volunteer vacation** Read **MORE** for pleasure **The leopard that lost its spots**
UNIT 11 He told us not to worry	• reported speech 1 • *want/ask/tell* someone to do something	• the environment	• say what you want people to do • read and write about ecology • listen to people talking about their heroes/heroines • talk about your heroes • write a leaflet **A Song 4 U** *We shall overcome*	Learn **MORE** through English **Energy and how to save it** **Science**
UNIT 12 California	• reported speech 2	• physical appearance **Sounds right** Word stress	• justify options • identify a person • read a description of Los Angeles • talk about Los Angeles • write about California **A Song 4 U** *California dreaming*	**Check your progress** Units 11 and 12 Learn **MORE** about culture **What a waste!** Read **MORE** for pleasure **The sound of California**

UNIT 7 I didn't use to like them

In this unit

You learn
- *used to*
- *so do I / neither do I*
- words for music

and then you can
- talk about what you used to do
- agree and disagree

48 **1 Read and listen to the dialogue.**

Claire Listen to that! How funny! I can't believe I used to like them.

Karen Who is it? I can't even remember them.

Rick Neither can I, and I had to listen to all of Claire's music when I was younger!

Claire It's *Don't Speak* by No Doubt.

Karen Oh, yes! That's what it is! I remember it now.

Oliver So do I. You used to play this all the time.

Claire Don't remind me! So, what else do we have here?

Oliver Pink, Outkast, I didn't use to like U2, but now I'm a big fan. In fact, I have a lot of their CDs. So, what are you into right now, Rick?

Rick I like hip-hop, especially classic stuff. I've just borrowed a bunch of my brother's old music. He used to spend his allowance on CDs, so he has a massive collection.

Claire I used to spend all my money on music, but now I've started collecting recorded books. You can get some amazing books!

Karen That's a great idea. Do you have *Lord of the Rings*?

Claire Yes, I have it on my MP3 player!

2 **Answer the questions.**

1 Who used to like No Doubt?
2 Who is a U2 fan?
3 What kind of music does Rick like at the moment?
4 What did Rick's brother use to do with his allowance?
5 What kind of collection does Claire have?
6 Has she always collected these things?

Get talking Talking about what you used to do

49 **3** **Listen and repeat.**

Interviewer Which TV show did you use to watch when you were 10?
Girl I used to watch *Charmed*!

Interviewer What did you use to like when you were younger?
Boy I used to like roller skating.

50 **4** **Match the questions and answers. Then listen and check.**

Questions

1 Dad, what music did you listen to when you were young?
2 Grandma, did you watch a lot of TV when you were a girl?
3 How did you use to spend your Saturdays, Mom?
4 Did you use to read a lot, John?
5 What was your favorite TV show back then, Natasha?

Answers

a Not really. I didn't like TV. I used to read.
b When I was younger, I used to watch *Buffy*!
c I used to like a band called Talking Heads.
d No, I used to go to the movies a lot.
e I used to go dancing on Saturdays!

5 **Work in pairs. Ask each other questions about what you used to do when you were younger.**

A What shows did you use to watch when you were younger?

B I used to watch cartoons all the time!

Language Focus

Vocabulary Music

1 **Number the musical styles. (1 = your favorite, 13 = your least favorite).**

☐ Dance

☐ R&B

☐ Folk

☐ Indie

☐ Hip-hop

☐ Opera

☐ Pop

☐ Jazz

☐ Country

☐ Blues

☐ Rock

☐ Heavy metal

☐ Classical

Get talking Agreeing and disagreeing

51

2 **Complete the dialogue with the phrases on the left. Listen and check.**

Oh, I do
Neither do I
So do I

Richard Do you like dance music?
Susan No, I don't.
Richard [1] .... , but my sister does. She's got hundreds of dance CDs.
Susan So what do you like?
Richard Well, post-punk bands like The Killers.
Susan [2] .... Have you got any Green Day CDs too?
Richard Yes, but I don't like them that much.
Susan [3] .... I really do.

3 **Work with a partner. Talk about the music you like or dislike.**

A What music do you like? / don't you like?
B I like / don't like ....
A So do I / Neither do I / Oh, I don't!

Grammar

used to

1 Complete the sentences. Then check against the dialogue on page 64.

You [1] .... this all the time.
He [2] .... his allowance on CDs, so he has a massive collection.
I [3] .... U2, but now I'm a big fan.

We use *used to / didn't use to* (+ verb) to talk about past habits.
The question (*Did you use to ...?*) is almost never used.

2 Put the words in the correct order.

1 live / there / I / to / used ......I used to live there......
2 to my school / used / go / She / to ....
3 the U.S. / to / We / live / used / in ....
4 to / vegetables / didn't / eat / I / use ....
5 have / didn't / to / I / use / my own bedroom ....
6 rock / didn't / like / My father / to / use / music ....

3 Complete with one of the phrases on the right.

used to eat
didn't use to eat
used to play
didn't use to play
used to go
didn't use to go
used to speak
~~didn't use to speak~~

1 I ......didn't use to speak...... English, but now I can say some things.
2 Steve .... the guitar at all, but now he plays very well.
3 My brother hates pizza, but when he was younger he .... it every day.
4 My mother .... Spanish, but now she's forgotten it.
5 We never go to the movies these days, but we .... every weekend.
6 My parents .... on vacation, but now they take a trip every year.
7 My favorite player is Alex Rodriguez. He .... for the Texas Rangers.
8 I .... spinach, but now I really love it!

4 Complete with *used to* or *didn't use to* and a verb from the box.

~~speak~~	eat	wear	live	be	do

1 My father ..used to speak.. some Japanese, but now he's forgotten it all.
2 My sister .... only white clothes, but now she likes to wear a lot of colors.
3 My brother .... a nervous person, but he isn't any more.
4 I .... any exercise, but now I run four times a week.
5 I .... vegetables, but now I eat them all the time.
6 We .... in a really small apartment, but now we live in a big house.

so do I / neither do I

5 **Complete the examples. Then check against the dialogue on page 64.**

Karen I remember it now.
Oliver [1] .... You used to play this all the time.
Karen I can't even remember them.
Rick [2] ...., and I had to listen to them when I was younger.

We use these phrases to agree with what another person says.

Simple present

If the other person says something affirmative, use: *So do I.*
If the other person says something negative, use: *Neither do I*

Other verbs

"**I'm** tired." "**So am I**." "I **can't** sing." "**Neither can I**." "I arrived late." "**So did I**."

6 **Complete the dialogue with these phrases.**

So do I.	So did I.	~~So can I.~~	So have I.
Neither do I.	Neither did I.	Neither can I.	Neither have I.

1 **A** Look! I can walk on my hands!
B ....So can I!....
2 **A** This homework's hard. I can't do it.
B ....
3 **A** I have a new bike.
B ....
4 **A** I always go to the movies on Fridays.
B ....
5 **A** We enjoyed ourselves at the party.
B ....
6 **A** I've never been to Europe.
B ....
7 **A** I didn't go out last night.
B ....
8 **A** My sister doesn't like rap.
B ....

7 **Complete the replies.**

1 I love spaghetti! ....So do I....
2 My brother has an MP3 player. ....
3 I went to Florida last year. ....
4 I don't know the answer. ....
5 I'm sorry, I can't go out tonight. ....
6 She didn't pass the test. ....
7 Mary can sing opera. ....

8 **Find sentences you agree with. Write *So ... I* or *Neither ... I*. Compare your answers with a partner's answers.**

1 I'm 16. ....
2 I'm not interested in sports. ....
3 I love football. ....
4 I watched TV last night. ....
5 I read magazines a lot. ....
6 I can't speak Spanish. ....
7 I didn't enjoy myself last night. ....
8 I can walk on my hands. ....
9 I think hip-hop is great. ....
10 I was in school yesterday. ....
11 I wasn't home on Sunday. ....
12 I haven't been to Canada. ....

Skills

Reading

52 **1** **Read and listen. Match the photos to the paragraphs.**

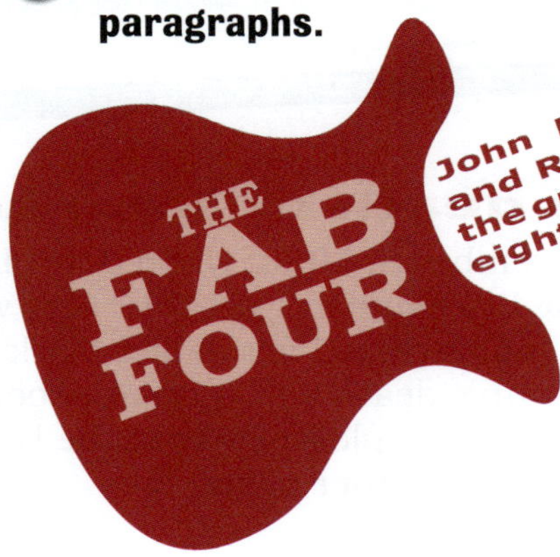

John Lennon, Paul McCartney, George Harrison and Ringo Starr—together they were the Beatles, the greatest band the world has ever seen. Here are eight of the most important events in their history.

A

B

C

Lennon and McCartney meet

On July 6, 1957, fifteen-year-old Paul McCartney first met John Lennon in Liverpool. John Lennon was on stage with his band The Quarry Men. Later in the evening, Paul played piano with the band. They thought he was so good that they asked him to join them.

The Beatles go to Germany [1] ☐

In August 1960, the Beatles went to Germany, where they played at Hamburg's Star Club until December 1. The band was made up of John Lennon (rhythm guitar/vocals), Paul McCartney (rhythm/vocals), George Harrison (lead guitar/vocals), and two other musicians on the bass and the drums.

The early hits [2] ☐

In summer 1962, a new drummer, Ringo Starr, joined John, Paul, and George. On October 11, 1962, the Beatles made their first appearance in the UK charts with "Love Me Do." In early 1963, their second single "Please Please Me" became their first number 1. The Beatles quickly followed this with another number 1 single, "From Me to You," and a number 1 album, also named *Please Please Me.*

The Beatles "invade" the U.S. [3] ☐

On February 7, 1964, 10,000 fans were at New York's Kennedy Airport to see Pan-Am flight PA101 land. On board were Paul, John, George, and Ringo. Four days later, the Beatles played their first American concert in Washington, D.C., to 8,600 screaming fans. More than 70 million Americans watched their performance on TV. On April 4, 1964, the top five singles in the United States were "Can't Buy me Love," "Twist and Shout," "She Loves You," "I Want to Hold your Hand," and "Please Please Me"—all of them were Beatles songs!

Sergeant Pepper's Lonely Hearts Club Band

On June 1, 1967, the Beatles released their eighth album, *Sergeant Pepper's Lonely Hearts Club Band.* Many people think this is the greatest of all their records. The album had the famous songs "She's Leaving Home," "When I'm Sixty-Four" and "Lucy in the Sky with Diamonds." It was also famous for its cover, which showed pictures of many of the band's idols.

The last show

On January 30, 1969, the Beatles played their last concert. It was a show on the roof of their record company in London. A large group of fans watched from the street below, but there were complaints about the noise from neighbors so the police arrived and stopped the show after only 42 minutes. Just over a year later, the band broke up.

Liverpool Echo

Crazed gunman charged

JOHN LENNON SHOT DEAD

JOHN LENNON, of the legendary Liverpool pop group, The Beatles, was shot dead in New York to-day by a crazed gunman.

The death of John Lennon 4 ☐

On December 8, 1980, when John Lennon was outside his home in New York City with his wife, Yoko Ono, a crazed fan called Mark Chapman shot him. John's death was a great shock all over the world. Now people knew that the Beatles would never play together again.

The release of *One* 5 ☐

In November 2000, a compilation of the Beatles' number 1 hits called *One* went straight to the top of the album charts. It was the fastest selling CD of the year and sold 320,000 copies in the first week. It also reached number 1 in many other countries around the world, including Germany, France, Spain, and Canada. It showed that the Beatles were still one of the biggest and most popular bands in the world.

2 Write the questions for these answers.

1 In Liverpool in 1957. *When and where did Paul first meet John?*
2 In August 1960. ....
3 "Please Please Me." ....
4 10,000. ....
5 In the summer of 1962. ....
6 On the roof of their record company. ....

Listening

1 CD 2

3 Paul Sacks and Sally Green are critics on the hit TV talent show *Superstar*. Listen and write the name of the person these sentences refer to (Jasmine or Dave).

1 Your voice needs a little more training. ....
2 You're not going to be our next superstar. ....
3 You look fantastic. ....
4 You gave it a try and that's what's important. ....
5 We certainly want to talk to you again. ....
6 You were out of tune. ....

Speaking

2 **4** **Work in pairs. Listen to these three performers and say what you think.**

Steve

Tina

Jeff

... looks fantastic / doesn't look like a pop star.
...'s got a beautiful / terrible voice / needs (doesn't need) training.
... is an excellent singer / was out of tune / has(n't) got what it takes.
... could be the next pop star / is never going to make it as a pop star / is(n't) on the way up.

Writing for your Portfolio

5 **Read the text and put the headings in the correct places.**

Career
Full name
Why I like her music
Born

My favorite singer

1 .... : Beyoncé Giselle Knowles

2 .... : Houston, Texas, in 1981

3 .... : Beyoncé rose to fame as a member of the band Destiny's Child. Their records sold millions of copies. In 2003 Beyoncé released her first solo album, *Dangerously in Love*. In 2006 she starred in the movies *The Pink Panther* and *Dreamgirls*.

4 .... : I love Beyoncé's music because she has an excellent voice and she is a great performer. My favorite Beyoncé songs are "Beautiful Liar" and "Irreplaceable."

6 **Now write a short summary about a pop star / band that you like.**

Learn MORE through English

Musical instruments

Key words

bamboo	folk music	metallic	an opening
binding	pear-shaped body	stringed	

1 **Look at the pictures of the four musical instruments.**

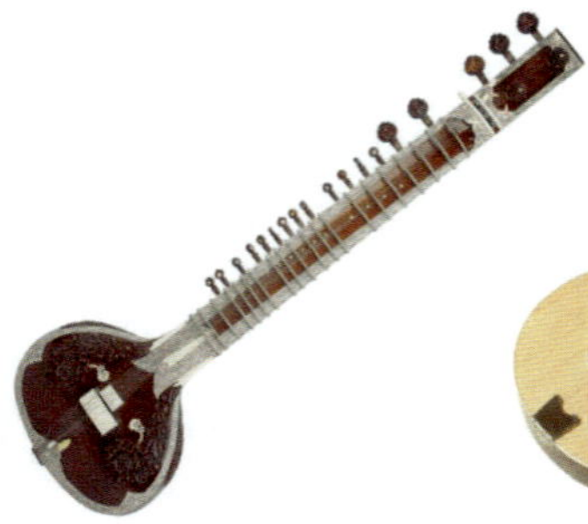
sitar

bouzouki

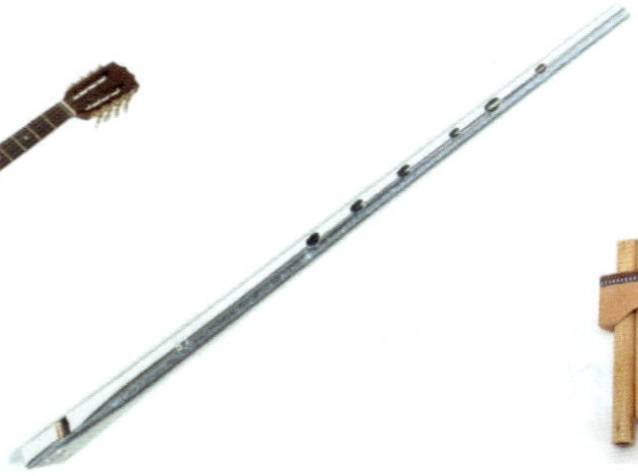
tin whistle

Andean flute

2 **Listen. Guess which instrument you hear. Write the numbers next to the names of the instruments.**

sitar .... bouzouki .... tin whistle .... Andean flute ....

3 **Write the names of the instruments from above into the text.**

The [1]... comes from Ecuador and is made of bamboo. It has 7 notes and is very easy to play. It often has a decorative binding.
The [2]... is important in modern Greek music as well as in other Balkan folk music. It is a stringed instrument with a pear-shaped body and a very long neck. The instrument has a sharp metallic sound.
The [3]... is a simple wind instrument with six holes. It can be made out of different kinds of metal. It is popular in traditional Irish music. Many children in Ireland play it because it doesn't cost much to buy and is easy to learn.
The [4]... is probably the best-known South Asian instrument in the West. It is an Indian classical stringed instrument. It became popular in the West when The Beatles used it in their songs. It is difficult to play.

4 **Folk music across the continents: The extracts you are going to hear are from Australia, Asia, North America, South America. and Europe. Try to guess where they are from.**

I think number one is from ...

I don't think so, it's from ...

5 **Look at the orchestra. Label the different sections.**

a) woodwind b) brass c) percussion d) string

5 **6** **Listen to the three following pieces of classical music. Which instruments can you hear?**

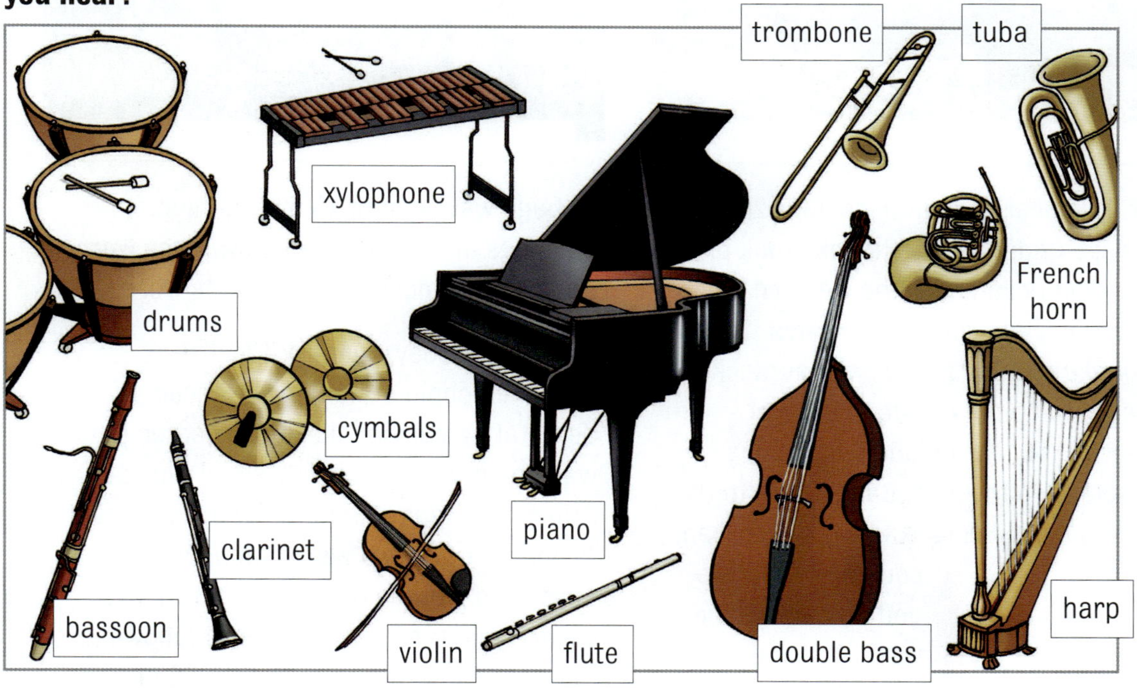

Mini-project Instruments from around the world

7 **Find out about two unusual instruments from your country. Write a short text about each one. Include a picture.**

UNIT 8 Natural disasters

1 **Read the text. Write the words in italics under the correct picture.**

http://www.historynews.net

Great disasters of the modern world

1 At 7:58 local time on December 26, 2004, a huge undersea earthquake took place in the Indian Ocean near the western coast of the Indonesian island of Sumatra. *The earthquake created tsunamis* that quickly traveled toward the coasts of several different countries, including Indonesia and Thailand to the east, Bangladesh to the north, and India, Sri Lanka, and the African countries of Kenya and Somalia to the west. Warnings were sent, but they arrived too late. Many of the coasts of these countries were hit by huge waves up to 15 meters high. Buildings and even *complete villages were destroyed.* Almost 300,000 people were killed.

2 On Tuesday, January 12, 2010, the people of Haiti experienced a devastating earthquake. Its epicenter was about 25 kilometers west of Port-au-Prince, the capital of Haiti. *Many important historical buildings were damaged or destroyed.* Dozens of strong aftershocks occurred in the days and weeks following the earthquake. More than 150,000 people lost their lives in the quake, which affected more than 3 million people. Many countries *sent aid to help the quake's survivors.*

In this unit

You learn

- *too / not ... enough*
- past passive
- words for catastrophes

and then you can

- express sympathy
- explain things in simpler words
- talk about where people were born

2 **Circle T (True) or F (False) for the sentences below.**

1 The Indian Ocean disaster took place in November 2004. T / F
2 Countries on four continents were affected by the Indian Ocean tsunami. T / F
3 Almost 300,000 people were killed. T / F
4 No one helped Haiti after the earthquake. T / F
5 Three million people were affected by the earthquake in Haiti. T / F

Get talking Expressing sympathy

6 **3** **Listen to the conversation. Complete it using the expressions on the right.**

A 1 ....
B Not very well.
A 2 ....
B It's about our dog.
A 3 ....
B It died yesterday.
A 4 ....

How are you, Sandra?

What about it?

Oh, I'm so sorry to hear that.

What's the matter?

4 **Choose situations. Act out dialogues like the one above.**

next weekend / I'm not allowed to come to your birthday party

tonight / I can't come to the movie

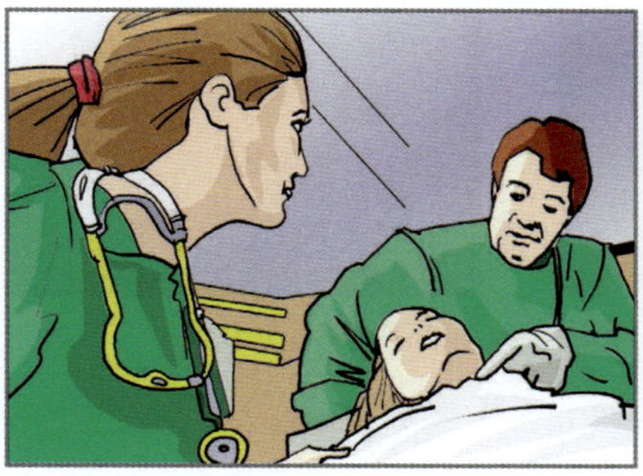

sister / was taken to the hospital yesterday

best friend / had a bike accident last week

new MP3 player / I broke it this morning

science test / I got a bad grade

Language Focus

Vocabulary Catastrophes

7 **1 Match the words with their definitions. Then listen and check.**

1 ☐ a lot of water covering a place that is usually dry.
2 ☐ a long time without rain.
3 ☐ a mass of mud and earth sliding down a mountain.
4 ☐ a mountain with a large hole in the top through which lava comes out.
5 ☐ a violent wind, especially found in the western Atlantic Ocean.
6 ☐ an extremely large wave that often happens after an earthquake.
7 ☐ when masses of ice and snow fall quickly down the side of a mountain.
8 ☐ when the earth shakes so strongly that sometimes houses are destroyed.
9 ☐ when a forest starts to burn.

a an earthquake

b an avalanche

c a volcano

d a flood

e a drought

f a tsunami

g a forest fire

h a mudslide

i a hurricane

Get talking Explaining things in simpler words

2 Cover up Exercise 1. In pairs, ask and answer questions.

A What's an "earthquake?"

B It's when the earth shakes so strongly that sometimes houses are destroyed.

B What's a "volcano?"

A A volcano? That's a mountain with hot lava inside. The lava comes out through a hole in the top.

Grammar

too / not ... enough

Warnings were sent but they	arrived **too** late.
	did**n't** arrive soon **enough**.

1 Complete the sentences with the adjectives on the right.

good
strong
~~tall~~
tired
late

1 He's not ....tall..... enough to get the apple from the tree.
2 We're too .... to see the movie. It started 15 minutes ago.
3 I'm not .... enough to be on the school football team.
4 She's too .... to do her homework now. She should go to bed.
5 You're not .... enough to lift this.

Past passive

2 Complete the examples with words from the box. Then check against the text on page 74.

were destroyed | were damaged | were hit
were sent | were killed

Many important historical buildings [1] .... or destroyed.
Warnings [2] ....
Many of the coasts of these countries [3] .... by huge waves.
Complete villages [4] ....
Almost 300,000 people [5] ....

3 Decide if the sentences are passive or active.

1 The hurricane destroyed thousands of homes. active
2 Breakfast is served until 10:00 a.m.
3 He was paid a lot of money for the photo.
4 We're not very happy with our room.
5 The teacher was 10 minutes late for class.
6 Children under 13 are not allowed in.

4 Write sentences with the past passive. Use the words below and *by*.

1 The email / write / Susan — The email was written by Susan.
2 The cupcakes / make / Fred — ....
3 The race / win / an Ethiopian — ....
4 The children / rescue / the police — ....
5 My website / design / my sister — ....
6 The pictures / paint / a famous artist — ....

Sounds right "r" sound

8 **5 Listen and repeat. Pay attention to the "r" sound.**

water earthquake destroyed
were erupted

9 **6 Listen and repeat the sentences.**

What's the matter?
The volcano erupted.
The buildings were destroyed.

Get talking Talking about when people were born

7 Write the number of the correct word in the pictures.

1 telephone
2 lightbulb
3 car
4 jeans
5 nuclear reactor
6 windshield wipers
7 dynamite
8 signal flare
9 dishwasher

8 Write the names of the inventors under the pictures. Then discuss your answers with a partner.

....

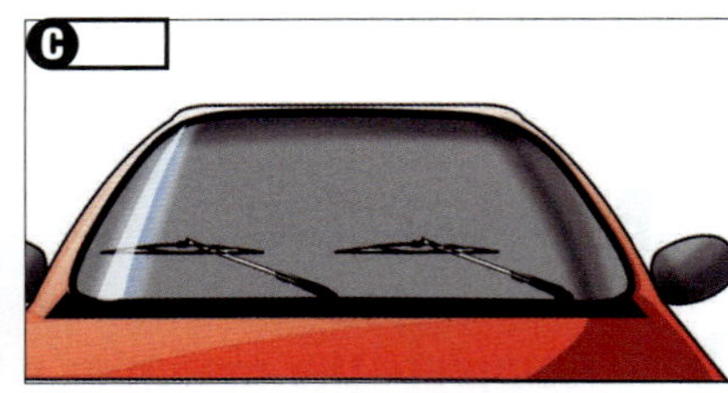

....

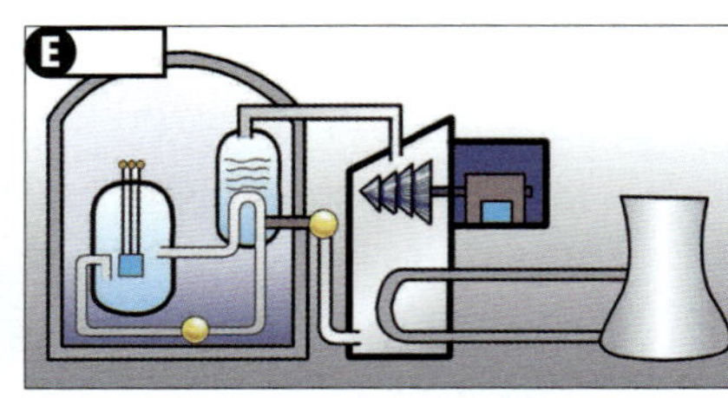

....

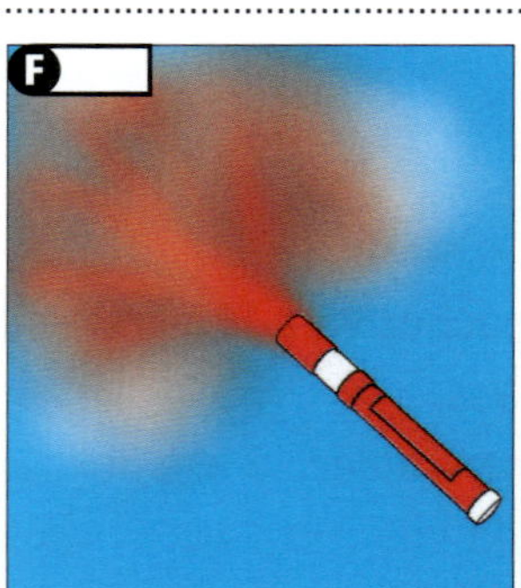

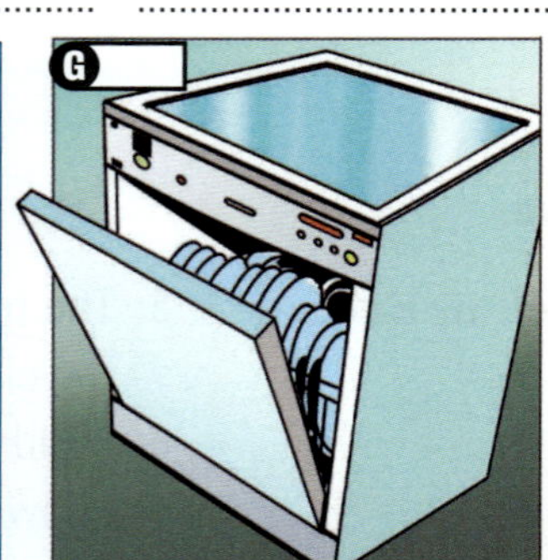

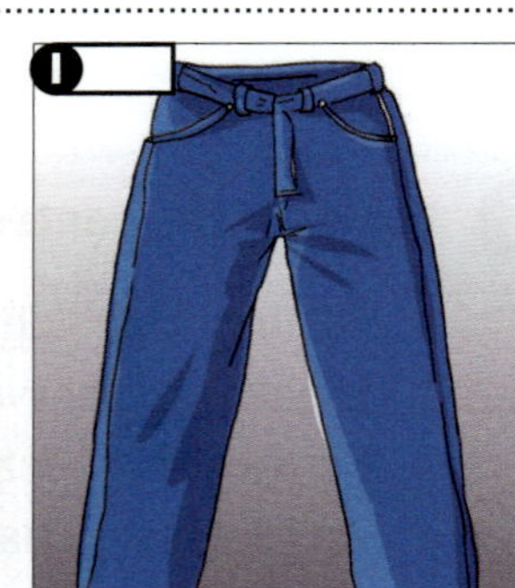

....

Mary Anderson *(born 1866 in Alabama, U.S.)*
Gottlieb Daimler *(born 1834 in Stuttgart, Germany)*
Josephine Cochrane *(born 1839 in Illinois, U.S.)*
Thomas Alva Edison *(born 1847 in Ohio, U.S.)*
Alfred Nobel *(born 1833 in Stockholm, Sweden)*
Levi Strauss *(born 1847 in Bavaria, Germany)*
Enrico Fermi *(born 1901 in Rome, Italy)*
Alexander Graham Bell *(born 1847 in Edinburgh, Scotland)*
Martha Coston *(born 1826 in Baltimore, U.S.)*

A I think the car was invented by Levi Strauss.

B I don't think so. I think it was invented by Gottlieb Daimler. / I think so, too.

Skills

Reading

1 Read the story.

CASTAWAY!

1 Chuck's plane was flying over the open ocean when a storm started. The plane ran into trouble when the storm got stronger. ☐

2 Eventually the plane crashed, but Chuck survived and he started swimming. ☐

3 On the island, Chuck learned how to open coconuts to get the milk and which berries were good to eat. ☐

4 After two or three weeks, he opened some of the packages that had washed ashore from the plane's wreckage. ☐

5 ☐ He amused himself by drawing a face on the ball with some of the blood. He gave the ball a name, too.

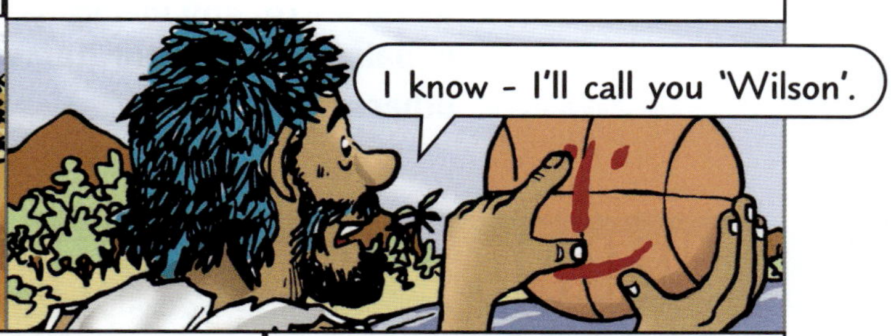

6 ☐ Wilson became Chuck's best friend. When Chuck escaped from the island on a raft six months later, he took Wilson with him.

7 After three days at sea, Wilson fell off the raft, but Chuck couldn't get him back. ☐

8 The following day, several months after the plane crash, a miracle happened. ☐

2 Write the letters of the extra sentences from the story in the boxes above.

A He also learned how to catch and cook fish.
B Chuck was rescued and taken back to the United States.
C After swimming for a long time, he reached a desert island.
D The pilot couldn't control the plane.
E Chuck gave up hope and just lay on the raft.
F He was surprised to find a ball in one of them.
G There was no one else to talk to, so Chuck talked to Wilson.
H While he was playing with the ball, Chuck fell down and cut his arm.

Listening

10 **3 Listen and find out how Sally and Tom James survived an earthquake. Complete the sentences.**

1 Sally was getting breakfast ready when ....
2 She looked out of the window and saw ....
3 Just before the big quake happened, she ....
4 She shouted and some men came. They ....
5 Tom was on his way ....
6 He stopped his car and ....
7 He ran as fast as he could until he ....
8 When he came back to his car, ...

Speaking

4 Imagine you are going to spend a year alone on a desert island. You are allowed to take a CD, a book, a DVD, and one other thing with you. Work in pairs. Choose your items and interview each other.

A What DVD are you going to take?

B I'm going to take *Titanic* because ...

Writing for your Portfolio

5 Read Paul's story about a forest fire near his home. Then complete it with these words.

then | ago | first | When | after | later

Two years [1]......, there was a bad forest fire near my town. At [2]......, it wasn't a problem, but [3]...... two days, the firefighters said people had to leave their houses. So we put some clothes into suitcases, and [4]...... we got in the car and drove to my grandparents' house. Three days [5]......, the fire stopped, and we drove back to our house. [6]...... we got there, we saw that the house was OK. We were happy to be back home again!

6 Write a story about someone who survived an earthquake. Use these verbs and the time words from Exercise 5.

to escape | to rescue | to crush | to shake | to collapse | a tremor | safe

Check your progress Units 7 and 8

1 Complete the words for kinds of music.

1 o _ _ _ _
2 f _ _ _
3 c _ _ _ _ _ _
4 i _ _ _ _
5 h _ _ _ _ m _ _ _ _
6 d _ _ _ _
7 b _ _ _ _

7

2 Read the descriptions and complete the words.

1 When there is no rain for a long time.
a d _ _ _ _ _ _
2 When the earth shakes.
an e _ _ _ _ _ _ _ _ _
3 When there is too much water.
a f _ _ _ _
4 Rocks and earth that fall down a mountain.
an a _ _ _ _ _ _ _ _
5 A violent wind.
a h _ _ _ _ _ _ _ _
6 A mountain with lava inside.
a v _ _ _ _ _ _

6

3 Complete the dialogue with the correct form of *used to*.

A Which school did you [1]........................ go to?
B I [2]........................ go to Mansfield School.
A I didn't [3]........................ like school, but this year I'm enjoying it.
B That's good. I hope I enjoy this school, too!

3

4 Rewrite the sentences using the simple past passive.

1 The hurricane destroyed the forest.
....
2 Van Gogh painted that picture.
....
3 Mark wrote these emails.
....
4 Sarah won the money.
....
5 A carpenter built these houses.
....

10

5 Complete the sentences with *too* or *not ... enough*.

1 He is not .... (good) to play for the basketball team.
2 We are .... (late) to see the movie. It started 10 minutes ago.
3 They were not .... (strong) to lift the boxes.
4 I was .... (tired) to stay up late.

4

6 Write the questions.

1 .... ?
He was born in 1972.
2 .... ?
Yes, I like jazz.
3 .... ?
I'm sad about my dog.
4 .... ?
It's when the earth shakes.
5 .... ?
I'm going to take a good book on vacation.

10

7 Complete the dialogues with the correct phrase.

Yes, I do.	So do I.	Do you want
What about	I like	Neither do I.

A Do you like U2?
B [1]..
A That's good. [2]..
B [3].. Green Day?
A I don't like them.
B [4]..
A [5]..................................... rock music these days. In fact, I'm going to a concert tomorrow. [6]..................................... to come?

6

What's the matter?	How are you?
Not great	I'm so sorry to hear that.

A [7]..., Sue?
B [8]..
A [9]..
B It's my grandmother. She's not very well.
A [10]...

4

TOTAL 50

My progress so far is ...

great. ☐ good. ☐ poor. ☐

Learn MORE about Culture

Manga!

1 **Discuss the questions below. Then read the text and answer the questions.**

Do you read manga comics?
Do you watch manga cartoons?
Who is your favorite manga character?

Did YOU know?

The word *manga* means "comic" in Japanese. Manga is written for both adults and children. The Japanese manga industry is HUGE. It is much bigger than the comic industry in the United States. Yearly sales of manga books and magazines in Japan total about $57 million.

So how did manga start? Cartoon drawing began in Japan almost 800 years ago. Artists drew manga on temple walls. These pictures were very similar to modern manga. In 1702, Shumboko Ono, a famous artist, made a book of these pictures and added captions. Manga artists started to use stories as well as illustrations.

These early comic books were called *Tobae*. They were the main form of literature in Japanese society. In 1947, Tezuka Osamu, a young medical student, created *New Treasure Island*. It was a great success. He became the father of "modern" manga. His most popular work is *Mighty Atom*. He also created *Astro Boy* and *Kimba the White Lion*.

Today in Japan, manga can be found on every street corner. Manga magazines contain at least 200-400 pages of manga in each issue. Hundreds of manga artists work individually or in small groups. Popular manga characters become TV cartoons or animated movies that are watched all over the world.

1 Is manga an old or new art?
2 What is *Tobae*?
3 Who became the father of modern manga?
4 How long are most manga magazines?

11 **2** **Listen and circle the correct word to complete the sentences below.**

1 *Naruto* comes from *a book / a magazine*.
2 *Naruto* takes place in a make-believe world with *five / six* countries.
3 Each country has a hidden *village / city* where Ninja live.
4 The name *Ninja* was the name of *teachers / spies* in the Samurai age.
5 Uzumaki Naruto is a *good / bad* student.
6 He has got an *eight-tailed / nine-tailed* fox inside his body.
7 He has *no / great* strength in times of danger.
8 Naruto's peers *don't possess / all possess* their own special powers.

3 **Over 2 U!** **Work in pairs and design a new manga character. Write an adventure for him or her, then present it to the class.**

MORE! Now you can watch Episode 4 of *The School Magazine*! DVD

HOW TO SURVIVE
Earthquakes

Do you ever get tired of all that advice you get in teen magazines? You know, stuff like how to survive at school, how to survive your parents, how to survive exams—things like that.
Well, I live in San Francisco and here we have something a bit more dangerous than parents and exams. They're called earthquakes and here's my survival guide.

HOW TO SURVIVE Earthquakes.

Stay calm. If you are inside, first of all get down on the floor and find some cover to protect you from falling objects, such as a heavy table or desk. Stay away from windows and objects that could fall on you.
If you are outside, move quickly away from buildings, streetlights, and trees. Try and find an open area.
If you are in a public building, do not rush to the door. That's what everyone else will do.
Never use an elevator during an earthquake.
After the quake has finished, watch out for aftershocks. These are follow-up quakes. They are usually smaller than the first one but they can still cause damage. They can cause things to fall down.
When you leave your house, make sure you are wearing shoes. They will be a lot of broken glass on the ground, for sure.

So how big was that quake?

The strength of each earthquake is measured on the Richter scale. It goes from 0 to 8.9. Here's a guide to what happens at different levels of the scale.

7.3–8.9

Total destruction;
roads break up and rocks fall.
The ground opens up.

6.2–7.3

People are starting to panic.
Buildings start to fall down.
Water is pushed out of rivers.

4.8–6.2

Now you are finding it difficult to stand up or walk.
Windows break and tiles fall off roofs.

4.3–4.8

If you were sleeping, you're not any more.
Dishes, doors, and trees shake and rock.

0–4.3

Lying on your bed upstairs, you are noticing the room is shaking a bit.
Lights start to swing inside.

For **MORE!** **Go to www.more-online.com/american and take a quiz on this text.**

UNIT 9 If I had the money …

In this unit

You learn

- second conditional
- *If I were you …*
- indefinite pronouns *everyone, someone, no one, anyone*
- words for computers

and then you can

- give advice
- talk about people
- talk about what you would do

12 **1 Read and listen to the dialogue.**

Oliver I really need to buy a new laptop, but don't have enough money.

Claire Why do you need a new laptop?

Oliver Well, if I had a built-in DVD player, I could watch my DVDs anytime, anywhere.

Karen If I were you, I'd use it to do more studying.

Oliver Oh, come on! No one has said anything about my grades. If anyone had, I would have started working harder.

Rick What about Mr. Sweeney?

Oliver What does he know? Everyone knows his classes are hard. I'd work harder if his classes were more interesting. Anyway, if I had this laptop here, I could study anywhere. Look, it's even got wireless LAN.

Karen If you need more money, why don't you get a job?

Oliver Doing what?

Karen Well, if you did a paper route, you'd earn some money.

Rick Hey, I have an idea. There's always someone who needs help with a computer. Why don't you make some money that way?

Oliver Good idea, Rick! Would you like another orange juice?

2 **Match the sentence halves.**

1 Oliver really wants a new laptop
2 He wants to watch DVDs and
3 Karen says he should
4 Oliver thinks he's working
5 If some classes weren't so boring,
6 Rick suggests he helps people
7 Oliver thinks this is

a do more studying.
b by fixing their computers.
c he would work harder.
d but he doesn't have enough money.
e a good idea.
f do a paper route.
g hard enough.

Get talking Giving advice

13 **3** **Listen and repeat.**

Girl 1 I need to get more exercise.
Boy 1 If I were you, I'd go running every morning.
Girl 1 Hmm. But I hate running!

Boy 2 I need some extra money.
Girl 2 If I were you, I'd get a job at the mall.
Boy 2 I can't, I'm too young.

4 **Match the expressions and the pictures.**

1 mow the lawn
2 take a dog for a walk
3 wash cars
4 fix computers
5 do a paper route
6 babysit

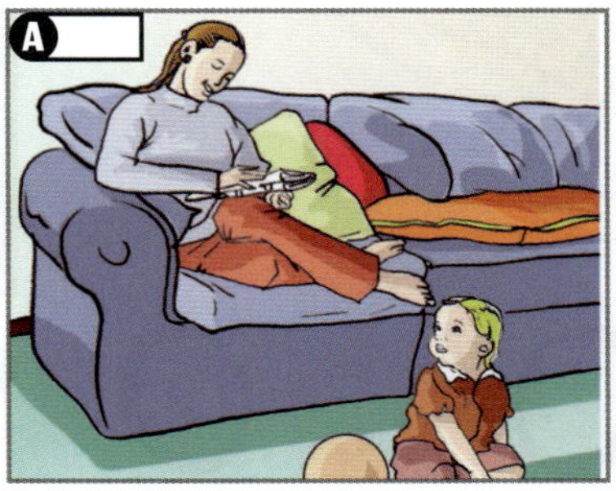
A

B

C

D

E

F

5 **Work in pairs. Make dialogues like those in Exercise 3.**

A I need ...

B If I were you, I'd ...

Language Focus

Vocabulary Computer words

14 **1 Write the correct number of the words in the pictures. Listen and check.**

1 CD-ROM	3 mouse	5 laptop	7 modem	9 printer
2 flat screen	4 keyboard	6 DVD	8 flash drive	10 speakers

A

B

C
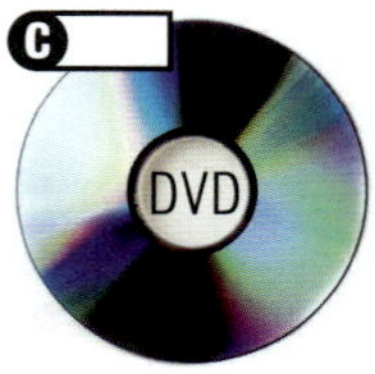

D

E
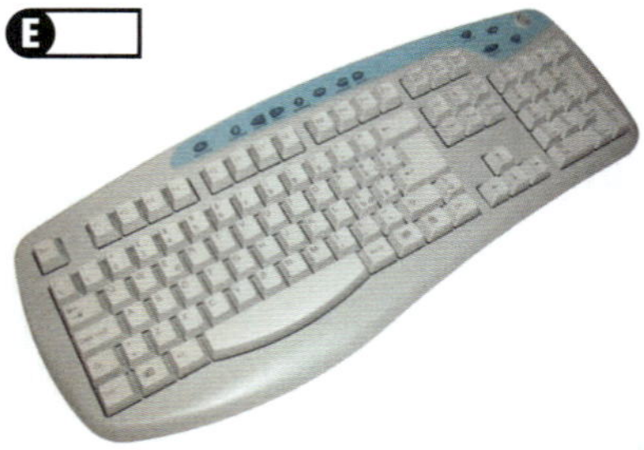

F

G

H

I

J
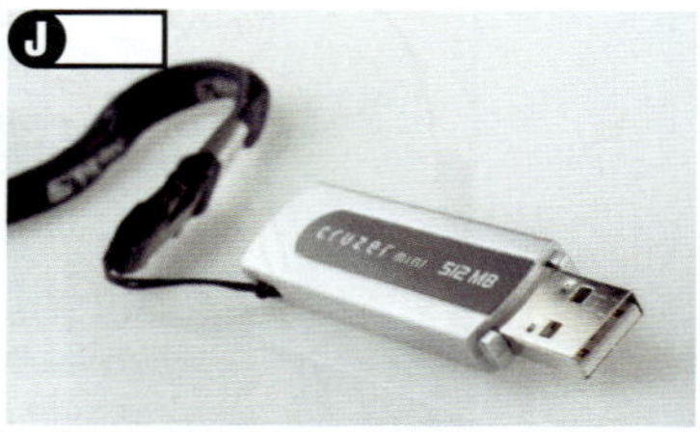

Get talking Talking about people

2 Work with a partner. Person A says one of the prompts, Person B finishes it. Then switch roles.

1 I know someone who ....
2 At our school, everyone ....
3 In our class, there isn't anyone who ....
4 In our country, no one ....
5 I don't know anyone who ....
6 At our school, no one is allowed to ....
7 In our class, there is someone who ....
8 In Australia, everyone ....

Grammar

Second conditional

1 Put the verbs into the correct places. Then check against the dialogue on page 84.

were | could watch | had | 'd earn | 'd work | did

1 I .... harder if his classes .... more interesting.
2 If you .... a paper route, you .... some money.
3 If I .... a built-in DVD player, I .... my DVDs anytime, anywhere.

The second conditional is used to talk about situations that are unreal.
Real: I don't have a notebook. I can't work anywhere.
Unreal: **If** I **had** a notebook, I **could** work anywhere.

Form:	**If clause**	**Main clause**
If + simple past	subject + would/wouldn't or could/couldn't + base form of the verb.	

2 Circle the correct word.

1 If I *have / had* more money, I'd buy it for you.
2 If you *go / went* to New York City, you'd learn a lot of English.
3 If it was my birthday today, *I'd get / I got* a lot of presents.
4 I would help you if I *didn't / wouldn't* have homework to do.
5 If he *would have / had* a girlfriend, he'd be very happy.
6 If there was a test tomorrow, I *wouldn't / didn't* pass it.

3 Write the verbs in the correct form.

1 I'd tell you the answer if I ....knew.... it myself! (know)
2 If I knew her phone number, I .... her. (call)
3 If today .... Sunday, I'd still be in bed! (be)
4 If you were my friend, you .... me. (help)
5 You'd have more money if you .... a job. (get)

Get talking Talking about what you would do

4 Work in pairs. Look at the prompts. Ask and answer.

A What would you do if you lost your key?

B I'd go to my friend's house. What would you do if …?

lost your key | were principal of your school | saw your teacher at the school dance
were angry with a friend | saw a famous person | felt sick

If I were you Giving advice

5 **Put the words in the correct order. Then check against the dialogue on page 84.**

If / you / I / I'd / to do more studying / were / use it

This is a special use of the second conditional: we use the phrase **If I were you** to introduce advice for another person.

A I've got toothache. **B If I were you,** I'd go see a dentist.

6 **Match the sentences.**

1 My tooth hurts. ....
2 My grades are really bad. ....
3 I need some exercise. ....
4 I'm really tired. ....
5 My dog's sick. ....
6 The television doesn't work. ....

a If I were you, I'd go for a run.
b If I were you, I'd take it to the vet.
c If I were you, I'd call the repair shop.
d If I were you, I'd go to the dentist.
e If I were you, I'd study harder.
f If I were you, I'd go to bed early.

Indefinite pronouns *everyone, someone, no one, anyone*

7 **Complete the sentences. Then check against the dialogue on page 84.**

[1] .... has said anything about my grades.
[2] .... knows his classes are hard.
There's always [3] .... who needs help with a computer.
If [4] .... had, I would have started working harder.

- Note that we can also say *everybody / somebody / nobody / anybody*.
- *no one / nobody* is only used with affirmative verb forms.
- *anyone / anybody* can be used with affirmative or negative verb forms:
  Anyone can do this. *I don't know anybody here.*

8 **Complete the sentences with the correct indefinite pronoun.**

1 We don't need a specialist for this job. ....Anyone.... can do it!
2 When I got to Mike's house, ... was there, so I went home again.
3 I can't do this. I want .... to help me.
4 Everybody is invited. .... can come!
5 I don't know .... who likes her.
6 It was a great party. Mike was there, Jenny was there—........................ was there!

Get talking Asking about how long

I were you | Everyone in my class

15 **9** **Complete the dialogue with the phrases above. Then listen and check.**

Craig I haven't finished my project yet.
Sonia Really? [1] .... has already finished.
Craig What can I do? If I had another two days, I'd do a great project.
Sonia If [2] ...., I'd research an idea on the Internet.
Craig Thanks. I'll do that.

Skills

Reading

1 Read the dilemmas and match them to the pictures.

Dilemma 1
Imagine your older brother asked you to give him an alibi for last night. He asked you to tell your parents he was with you. What would you do?

Dilemma 2
Imagine someone broke the classroom window when your teacher wasn't there. When she returns, she asks you who it was. What would you do?

Dilemma 3
Imagine you were walking down the street and you found a wallet on the ground. What would you do?

Listening

16 **2 Listen to Carla and Derek talking about the dilemmas in Exercise 1. Circle T (true) or F (false).**

1 Carla has two brothers. T / F
2 Carla would always give an alibi. T / F
3 Derek has a good relationship with his brother. T / F
4 Carla would definitely tell the teacher. T / F
5 Derek wouldn't tell the teacher anything. T / F
6 Derek thinks it would be unfair if the teacher asked him. T / F
7 Carla would keep the wallet. T / F

Reading and speaking

3 **Do the questionnaire. Put a check next to your answers. Then discuss them.**

1 Imagine you were at a party. You took a picture off the wall to look at it. You dropped it and it broke. No one saw you do it. What would you do?

- ☐ I'd offer to fix it.
- ☐ I'd put it back on the wall and hope no one would notice.
- ☐ I'd leave it on the floor and go back to the party.

2 Imagine a friend of yours had some new glasses and you thought they looked ridiculous. If your friend asked you for your opinion, what would you do?

- ☐ I would say I liked my friend's old glasses better.
- ☐ I would say they looked ridiculous.
- ☐ I would say they looked good.

3 Imagine you played on the school football team and the team was in the championship. On the day of the game, you woke up and your leg was hurting. What would you do?

- ☐ I'd want to play, so I wouldn't say anything.
- ☐ I'd talk to the coach and ask for advice.
- ☐ I wouldn't play.

4 Imagine you had $150 to buy a new bike, but your best friend called you and asked if he could borrow $150. What would you do?

- ☐ I'd lend him the money and buy a cheaper bike.
- ☐ I wouldn't give him the money.
- ☐ I'd tell him to talk to his parents about the problem.

5 Imagine you were having dinner at your friend's house and his dad served you some vegetables that you really didn't like. What would you do?

- ☐ I'd tell him that I didn't like them.
- ☐ I'd leave them on my plate.
- ☐ I'd hide them in my pockets.

A Song 4 U If I were you

17 **4 Listen and complete the song using the words on the left.**

sad
would
were
goodbye (x2)
weren't
road
had
wheel

Oh my dear, if I [1]............. you
Then I wouldn't feel all blue,
Then I wouldn't feel all [2]............. ,
And I wouldn't feel so bad.

Chorus:
Turn the [3]............. back
Go and try
It won't work
I tell you [4].............
Turn the wheel back
Go and try
Everyone has got to say
Goodbye.

If I [5]............. another day,
I would surely like to stay.
If I had another year,
I [6]............. surely spend it here.

If my life [7]............. all mapped out,
If I had some little doubt
Where my [8]............. is leading to,
I would surely stay with you.

Oh my dear, if I were you,
Then I wouldn't feel all blue.
Life goes on, we wave [9]............. ,
Meet again maybe some day.

Writing for your Portfolio

5 Write dilemma questions with three answers. Put all the dilemmas together and make a class questionnaire. Compare your answers.

Example:
Imagine you borrowed a CD from a friend and you lost it.
What would you do?
I would buy another one.
I would hope he / she forgot about it.
I would say I was sorry.

Number challenges

Key words

divide by	subtract	sum (or total)	row	horizontal
multiply by	a half	digit	column	
add (up)	circular	square	diagonal	

18 **1** **Work in pairs. Try to find the answers to these questions. Take notes. Then listen and check.**

a What's 50 divided by a half?

b If there are three pizzas and you take away two, how many do you have?

c A man lives next to a circular park. In the park, there are exactly 356 trees. Every morning, the man walks around the park. It takes him 80 minutes to walk around the park in a clockwise direction, but 1 hour 20 minutes to walk around it in a counterclockwise direction. Why?

d You are driving a train from New York City to Philadelphia. The train leaves at 11:00 and travels for two hours. There is a 20-minute stop in Newark and a half hour stop in East Brunswick. Then the train continues for another three hours. What's the driver's name?

e Three friends have a meal at a restaurant. The check is $30, so each of them pays $10. Ten minutes later (the friends are still in the restaurant) the waiter notices a mistake on the check. He charged $5 too much. So he takes five one-dollar bills from the till to give to the three friends. On his way to their table, the waiter decides to keep $2 as a tip because it is difficult to divide $5 by 3. He gives each of the friends $1 back. So each of the friends paid $9. The waiter kept $2, so the total is $29. What happened to the missing $1?

Math

2 **Practice this magic number trick yourself first. Then show it to a friend.**

1 On a piece of paper, write the number NINE (in words). Do not show it to your friend. Fold the paper and put in an envelope. Seal the envelope and give it to your friend. Ask him/her not to open it yet.

2 Tell your friend to take a piece of paper and write down the last two digits of their phone number. Tell them to add the number of dollars (or yen, yuan, euros, pesos, or whatever the currency in your country is) they have in their pocket to the last two numbers of their phone number.

3 Tell your friend to add his/her age and the number of their house or apartment.

4 Tell them to subtract the number of brothers and sisters they have.

5 Tell them to subtract 12. Then add their favorite number.

6 Your friend should now multiply the total by 18.

7 Tell your friend to add up all the digits in the final total.

8 If the answer is more than 1 digit long, your friend should add up the digits again. (If necessary, your friend should do this until there is only one digit left).

9 Tell your friend that you know exactly what the answer is. Ask them to open the envelope and check.

19 **3** **Mini-project** Make a magic square for someone's birthday

1 If you are looking for a nice birthday present for someone, you can easily create a magic square for them. The person must be older than 22. Lisa made this card for her mother, who is 37. Add up the numbers in every row and in every column. Then check the diagonal lines in the middle. Find out if Lisa got it right.

8	11	17	1
16	2	7	12
3	19	9	6
10	5	4	18

2 Can you create a magic square for someone? Remember, though, the person has to be over 22 years old.

3 To check and find out how you can do this, listen and take notes.

UNIT 10 Into the wilderness

1 **Oliver is going to Botswana with his parents. Read the emails he writes to his friend Sam back home.**

Hi Sam,
I'm going to spend my summer vacation this year in Botswana with my parents. "Where's that?" you'll ask. I'll tell you in a minute because I've checked it out. The story is that Mom and Dad are going to Botswana to show people how to use the water they have in a better way. Yesterday, they told me that I'm coming, too. They have already had all their equipment flown out to Botswana. We're going next week, can you imagine? I'm pretty excited. It must be amazing there. I still have a lot to do though. Later today, I'm going to have my passport photo taken! #:-O)
See you,
Oliver

Botswana. Facts for my friends:
It's not in South Africa, it's in Africa just north of South Africa in fact. It's almost as big as the state of Texas. Any idea how many people live there? Well, I'll tell you: there are one-and-a-half million people! Imagine that. There can't be a lot of towns and cities. As big as Texas, but only 1.5 million people. There are about 25 million in Texas. Most of Botswana is desert, so water must be a very important thing. And the official language is English! Most people speak English and Setswana. So, that's enough for now. Look at the map. Check out where Gabarone is. That's the capital. It's where we're going to fly first.

In this unit

You learn
- make deductions
- causative *have*
- words for vacations

and then you can
- give reasons
- talk about vacation plans
- make deductions

2 Answer the questions below.

1 Why are Oliver and his family going to Botswana?
2 What does Oliver have to do before he goes to Botswana?
3 How does Botswana compare to the state of Texas (size and number of people)?
4 Why is water so important to people in Botswana?
5 What language(s) do people in Botswana speak?
6 What is the capital of Botswana?

Get talking Giving reasons

20
3 Listen and repeat.

A Where do you want to go on vacation this year?
B I want to go to Africa.
A Why?
B To go on safari.

A Are you going on vacation this year?
B Yes, we want to go to Mexico.
A Why?
B To relax on a beach.

21
4 Match the pictures with the activities. Then listen and check.

1 go on safari
2 go surfing
3 go camping
4 go mountain climbing
5 see the Statue of LIberty
6 go hiking
7 go skiing
8 relax on a beach
9 go horseback riding

5 Check the activities you want to do on vacation and decide which of the places below is the best place to do them. Work with a partner and make up similar dialogues to those in Exercise 3.

Africa Mexico Canada Australia Japan the U.S.

Language Focus

Vocabulary Vacation words

book
buy
look at
make
find out
rent
check out
take

22 **1 Listen and complete the phrases using the words on the left.**

1	.... a flight	5	.... a map of the area
2	.... a trip	6	.... the area .... on the web
3	.... a hotel reservation	7	.... what to do there
4	.... a car	8	.... a dictionary

2 Work with a partner. Student A: Close your book. Student B: Ask four questions to see how many verbs Student A can remember from Exercise 1. Switch roles.

A What's number 3?

B make a hotel reservation

Get talking Talking about vacation plans

surfing
booked
vacation
made
camping

23 **3 Listen and complete the dialogue with the correct words.**

A Where are you going on [1]...................... this year?
B We're going camping near the coast. I'm going to learn [2]...................... and windsurfing.
A Cool! Have you [3]...................... a flight?
B Yes, we have.
A Have you [4]...................... a hotel reservation?
B No, we haven't. It's a [5]...................... trip!

Sounds right Question intonation

24 **4 Listen and repeat.**

A Do you have any plans for your vacation?
B Yes, I have.

A Have you booked your flight yet?
B No, I haven't.

5 Work with a partner. Talk about your vacation plans. Use the language below.

A Do you have any plans ...

A Have you ... yet?

A Have you ...

B Yes, I'm going ...

B Yes, I have.

Grammar

Making deductions

1 **Complete the sentences with one word. Then check against the text on page 94.**

I'm so excited. It [1] .... be amazing there.
There are only one-and-a-half million people! Imagine that. There [2] .... be a lot of towns and cities.

When you make an affirmative deduction, use *must*:
He won the game. He **must be** happy. (I'm sure that he is happy.)

When you make a negative deduction, use *can't*:
He lost the game. He **can't be** happy. (I'm sure that he is not happy.)

2 **Circle the correct option.**

1 She has 30 birthday cards. She *must / can't* have a lot of friends.
2 He's calling from a pay phone. His cell phone *must / can't* be broken.
3 She doesn't speak Spanish. She *must / can't* be from Peru.
4 She looks young. She *must / can't* be more than 20.
5 He's got hundreds of CDs. He *must / can't* love music.
6 He didn't eat anything. He *must / can't* like pizza very much.

3 **Write deductions about these people. Use the words below to help you.**

1 happy
He must be happy

2 old enough
....

3 very intelligent
....

4 hungry
....

5 Italian
....

Get talking Making deductions

4 **Work in pairs. A: Choose sentences from column A. B: Choose a suitable answer from column B. Switch roles.**

A	B
I haven't eaten for six hours.	You've already eaten two. You can't be hungry.
I have lost the CDs I bought yesterday.	You must be hungry.
Linda told me she's broken my MP3 player.	You must be angry.
I'd like another burger.	You must be sad.
Can you get me another sweater, please?	You've already got three. You can't be cold.

Causative *have*

5 **Put the words in the correct order. Then check against the text on page 94.**

Going / passport photo / to / taken / have
They / flown out / had / their equipment / have / to Botswana

We use this structure to say that another person does/did the action for us.
I had my photo **taken** last week. (= I did not take it myself, another person took it)
Form: Person + (form of the verb *have*) + object + past participle of the main verb.

6 **Complete the phrases with one of the verbs on the right.**

1 to have your hair ....
2 to have your room ....
3 to have your hair ....
4 to have your bike ....
5 to have a window ....
6 to have a carpet ....

cut
painted
fixed (2)
changed
dyed

7 **Look at the pictures and talk about what David and Hannah have had done.**

A He's had his hair cut.
B ....
C She's had her room painted.
D ....

Infinitives of purpose

8 **Join the sentences together. Use *to* and *because*.**

1 Mary bought a new dress. She wants to wear it to the party.
Mary bought a new dress to wear to the party.
Mary bought a new dress because she wants to wear it to the party.

2 John called me. He wanted to invite me to the party.
....
....

3 Ben bought a new bike. He wanted to get some exercise.
....
....

4 I went to the newsstand. I wanted to get the new *City Review* magazine.
....
....

5 Jill turned off the TV. She wanted to read a book.
....
....

Skills

Reading

1 Find out what happened to Oliver on his trip.

From: Oliver
To: Sam
Attachment:
Subject: News

Hi Sam,
Tuesday. Tomorrow we're going to fly from Gabarone to Maun. Mom's going to do some work with people in the desert for a few days, and Dad's going to take me to the Okavango Delta for six days. The Okavango is a large wetland. I hope we see lions, leopards, buffalo, rhinos, elephants, giraffes, zebras, and crocodiles. I'm glad I brought my new camera with me. We're going to fly into the delta tomorrow on a small plane.
Bye for now,
Oliver

From: Oliver
To: Sam
Attachment:
Subject: News

Hi Sam,
Still Tuesday. You know what happened at lunchtime? The window of my room in the hotel was open and I saw a man on the balcony next to our room. He had a black beard and was wearing sunglasses. He was making a phone call. I didn't hear everything, but one thing was clear: the man wanted to kill a leopard. :-o He said: "Okay. Let's meet in two days' time at Chitabe." That's a camp—and it's where we're going!
CU
Oliver

From: Oliver
To: Sam
Attachment:
Subject: News

Hi Sam! Today's Wednesday. The alarm clock rang at 5:30 this morning! "Get up, Oliver!" Dad said with a smile. "Today we're going to see the big five: a lion, a rhino, an elephant, a buffalo, and a leopard!" he said. Dad looked like a five-year-old at an amusement park!
The flight was only half an hour, and when I looked down everything looked amazing.
In the afternoon, we had our first trip in a Land Rover. First, we saw lots of elephants. When they slowly walked away, I saw some giraffes and zebras on the other side of the river. They were so cute, especially the young ones! I took a lot of photos and then I suddenly saw my first leopard! What a cat!

2 Read the text in Exercise 1 again. Then answer the questions.

1 What is the Okavango Delta? ....
2 Which animals did Oliver hope to see in the delta? ....
3 What did Oliver hear in the hotel at lunchtime? ....
4 What did the man look like? ....
5 How long did the flight into the delta take? ....
6 What animals did Oliver see on his first trip into the delta? ....

Listening

25 **3 Listen to Sam talking about Oliver's emails. Then complete the sentences.**

broken arm / man had a cut on his head	arrested two men	landed on its roof	control
the hotel / wanted to kill the leopard	the life of a leopard	~~wanted to kill a leopard~~	
wanted to come to their camp	a black car	the car before	

1 Oliver told Alex, the driver, about a man who *wanted to kill a leopard*
2 Oliver told Alex that the man ......
3 On the afternoon drive Alex suddenly saw ......
4 The other guide had never seen ......
5 The driver of the black car lost ......
6 The black car rolled over and ......
7 One man had a ......, and the other ......
8 The man with the broken arm was the man from ...... who ......
9 The park rangers ......
10 Alex said that Oliver had saved ......

Writing for your Portfolio

4 Read the summary of part of Oliver's adventures in Botswana. Check it against the text on page 99. Find and correct three mistakes.

On Thursday Oliver went to camp Chitabe in the Okavango Delta with his dad to see the animals. The day before they went, Oliver heard three men talking about killing an elephant at the camp. He was worried. At the delta they saw lots of amazing animals, including a leopard.

5 Look at the script of the story. Write a summary of what happened next. Don't write more than 50 words.

Writing tips Summary writing

- Look at the text and underline the important information. This is the information that you really need to retell the story.
- Think about ways that you can make this information shorter. What words can you leave out?
- Rewrite the sentences. Don't use the sentences from the text.
- When you have finished, read your summary again to make sure that it is clear and easy to understand.

Check your progress Units 9 and 10

1 Reorder the letters and write words for parts of the computer.

1 semou ....
2 medom ....
3 nterpri ....
4 krsespea ....
5 boyekrda .... ☐ 5

2 Complete the phrases.

1 book a f _ _ _ _ _
2 plan a t _ _ _
3 make a r _ _ _ _ _ _ _ _ _ _
4 look at a m _ _
5 buy a d _ _ _ _ _ _ _ _ _ ☐ 5

3 Complete the dialogue with *everyone, someone, no one,* and *anyone*.

A [1]............ knows Marco. He's very popular.
B When I arrived at this school last year. I didn't know [2]............... . Marco was the first person I spoke to.
A [3]............... likes their first day at school.
B It was terrible. I really needed [4]............... to talk to and I found Marco! ☐ 4

4 Complete using the second conditional.

1 I .... (go) if I ....(know) the address.
2 If they .... (have) more money, they .... (buy) the house.
3 If she ....(get) a job, she .... (be) happier.
4 We .... (help) them if they .... (need) it.
5 He ...... (learn) more English if he .... (go) to New York.
6 If they .... (speak) more clearly, we .... (understand) them. ☐ 6

5 Complete the sentences with a verb and the causative *have*.

1 He .... his hair .... (cut) yesterday.
2 We .... our photos .... (take) there.
3 She .... her bag ....(steal)
4 They .... their car .... (check) today.
5 I always .... my papers .... (deliver)
6 She .... her bike .... (fix) yesterday. ☐ 6

6 Write advice using *If I were you,...* and the verbs below.

1 .... (do a paper route)
2 .... (go out more)
3 .... (go running)

☐ 6

7 Write a deduction for each sentence.

1 I haven't had lunch. (hungry)
....
2 I've just passed my exams. (happy)
....
3 He's just lost his job. (upset)
....
4 She's just opened the window. (hot)
....
5 You slept until 1:00 p.m. (tired)
....

☐ 10

8 Complete the sentences using *to* or *because*.

1 My dad lent me money .... I want to buy a car.
2 I went to the library .... I wanted a book.
3 He turned off the TV .... he needed to work.
4 My friend called .... invite me to the movies. ☐ 8

TOTAL ☐ 50

My progress so far is ...

great! ☐ good. ☐ poor. ☐

Volunteer vacation

1 **Read about *summer volunteer programs for teens.* Then answer the questions.**

It is becoming more and more common for teenagers to spend their summer vacation helping other people.

Landmark Volunteers is one organization that helps teenagers find the right volunteer vacation for them. It gives high-school students aged 14 and a half and older opportunities to build homes, clear and restore nature trails, help children with disabilities, and much more.

Most of the programs run for one or two weeks. Teenagers can choose to go on one of 63 programs all around North America. They work as part of a team with a group of 12 other high-school students from around the country.

Do you know?

During the summer, many American students choose to travel or do volunteer work. Sometimes students join a program such as Landmark Volunteers, or BUNAC.

1 What is the name of the organization that can help teens find a volunteer vacation?
2 How long are the summer programs?
3 How old do you have to be to volunteer?
4 What are some of the things volunteers can do?

26 **2** **Listen and write the name of the correct organization under each photo.**

Global Works Travel   Landmark Volunteers   Bunac

Organization: ....

Organization: ....

Organization: ....

3 **Over 2 U!** **What would you do if you had the opportunity? Interview your classmates and write down who would do what.**

Would you like to ..?
Yes, I would. No, I wouldn't. I would like to ...

MORE! Now you can watch Episode 5 of *The School Magazine*! DVD

THE LEOPARD THAT LOST ITS SPOTS

If you count a leopard's spots
You'll find that it's got lots and lots.
(Only other leopards know
Just how many spots they grow.)

Lenny was a leopard small
Who one day heard his mother call:
"Lenny's sick! What has he got?
He's lost his biggest, blackest spot!"
Poor Lenny hunted high and low,
Just where it was he didn't know.
The other leopards looked around,
But still the spot could not be found.

Now in the jungle lived a man,
And down to him young Lenny ran.
He told him of his missing spot.
The man said, "I know what I've got!"
He went into his grassy den
And came out with a little pen.

Soon Lenny ran back home again,
His visit had not been in vain.
Upon his back, what do you think?
A brand new spot in thick, black ink!
The leopards thanked the man who plotted
To make their Lenny fully spotted!

For MORE! Go to www.more-online.com/american and take a quiz on this text.

UNIT 11 He told us not to worry

In this unit

You learn

- reported speech 1
- *want/ask/tell* someone to do something
- words for the environment

and then you can

- say what you want people to do

27 **1 Read and listen to the dialogue.**

Karen Did you hear about the park?

Claire No. What about it?

Karen They say that they want to cut down some of the trees and make it much smaller. They want to build a car park and they need part of the park for the entrance, the part near South Street.

Claire But that means we can't play there any more. What can I do to help?

Karen I want you to go and talk to other people in the park. Then we can decide on a plan of action.

(*The next day*)

Karen Oliver and I went to the city council yesterday and talked to an official there. He told us they are going to do it. He told us not to worry. He said that we'll still have half the park to play in!

Claire That's true, but there's no playing field in the other half.

Karen I know! Work's going to start in a month. He asked us to support the city council. But I want to organize a protest march through the park.

Rick What about a petition? We can ask people to sign it!

Karen Good idea!

2 Match the sentence halves.

1 Karen says that they want to cut down
2 She says that they want to build
3 Karen says that she
4 Oliver and Karen go to the city council
5 The city planner wants them to
6 They want to write a petition,

a wants Claire to talk to other people in the park.
b and speak to a city planner there.
c trees and make the park smaller.
d support the city council.
e and organize a protest march.
f a car park.

Get talking Saying what you want people to do

28 3 Listen and repeat.

A I want you to do something for me.
B What is it?
A I want you to mail a letter.
B OK, I'll do that right away.

A I want you to do something for me.
B What is it?
A I want you to come to the grocery store with me.
B I'm sorry, I can't. I have to do my homework.

29 4 Match the phrases with the pictures. Listen and check.

1 do the dishes
2 buy me an ice-cream cone
3 help me with my homework
4 mail a letter
5 go grocery shopping
6 lend me some money

5 Work with a partner. Make dialogues like the ones from Exercise 3. Use ideas in the pictures above.

Language Focus

Vocabulary The environment

1 **Match the phrases and the pictures.**

HOW GREEN ARE YOU?

A 1 Save water.

B ____ Don't take plastic bags to your supermarket. **BRING A BASKET.**

C ____ Ride your bike or walk.

D ____ Recycle glass bottles.

E ____ DON'T BE A LITTERBUG

F ____ RECYCLE PAPER.

2 **Read the questionnaire and circle your answers. See how "green" you are.**

What's your green score?

1 I (a) always (b) sometimes (c) hardly ever (d) never save water.

2 I (a) always (b) sometimes (c) hardly ever (d) never recycle glass jars.

3 I (a) never (b) hardly ever (c) sometimes (d) always throw paper and plastic bottles on the ground.

4 When leaving the beach I (a) never (b) hardly ever (c) sometimes (d) always leave litter behind.

5 I (a) always (b) sometimes (c) hardly ever (d) never put paper into special containers to be recycled.

6 I (a) never (b) hardly ever (c) sometimes (d) always ask my parents to drive me short distances.

Scores

If you circled (a) at least four times: You are very "green."

If you circled (b) at least four times: You are mostly "green." Keep it up.

If you circled (c) at least four times: You probably know what you should do, but you are too lazy.

If you circled (d) at least four times: You are a litterbug. You are not "green" at all.

Grammar

Reported speech 1

1 **Look at the dialogue on page 104 and complete the examples.**

He [1] .... are going to do it.
He [2] ....'ll still have half the park to play in.

2 **Complete the rule with *say* or *tell*.**

When we report what people say, we often use the verbs *say* and *tell*.
[1] .... is not followed by an object.
[2] .... is followed by an object.

Make sure you change the pronoun.
Helen said, "**You** look sad." = She said that **I** look sad.
Bob said, "**We** might be late" = He said **they** might be late.
Trevor said, "It's **my** birthday." = He told us that it's **his** birthday.

3 **Circle the correct option.**

1 He *says / says me* that he doesn't speak English very well.
2 They *told / told us* they were Spanish.
3 She *told / told her* she wasn't coming.
4 He *says / says him* he wants more French fries.

4 **Complete the sentences.**

1 "I'm hungry," says Paul.
Paul says that ..he is hungry..
2 "We're going home," Jenny tells me.
Jenny tells me ...
3 "I'm not happy," says Sue.
Sue ...
4 "You look like my sister," the girl tells me.
The girl ...
5 "You are tired!" she tells us.
She ...
6 "They are going to sell the house," May says. May ...

want/ask/tell someone to do something

We often use the verb *want* with an object pronoun + *to*.

I want **you** to go and talk to other people in the park.
I **don't** want **you** to tell anyone.
The verbs *ask* and *tell* have a similar construction in the negative form. Note the position of *not*.
He told us **not to** worry.
He **asked** me **not to** tell anyone.

5 **Match the sentences and pictures.**

1 He wants you to take him for a walk.
2 I want you to go to sleep now.
3 He asked me to marry him.
4 She asked me not to drive so fast.
5 She told him not to run.
6 He told me to be quiet.

6 Put the words in order to make sentences.

1 help / he / to / him / asked / me — *He asked me to help him.*
2 buy / she / to / some / him / milk / asked — ....
3 say / they / not / me / to / anything / asked — ....
4 I / for / her / to / told / me / wait — ....
5 not / we / them / to / anything / touch / told — ....
6 with / he / wanted / to / me / him / go — ....

7 Make the sentences negative.

1 I want you to turn off the TV. — *I don't want you to turn off the TV.*
2 He told me to leave. — ....
3 We asked them to be there at 5:00 p.m. — ....
4 She told us to buy some bread. — ....
5 Dave wants us to arrive early. — ....
6 I told them to play in the yard. — ....

30

8 Complete the dialogue with the phrases on the right. Listen and check. Then act it out.

Sandra Gerry?
Gerry What is it, Sandra?
Sandra I want you [1]..........
Gerry What is it?
Sandra [2].......... me they are planning to build a highway through our neighborhood.
Gerry Through our neighborhood? No way!
Sandra Exactly. [3].......... work's going to start next month. That's why [4].......... to help me.
Gerry Help you with what?
Sandra We want to [5].......... a petition and [6].......... leaflets to all the people in the neighborhood.
Gerry That's a great idea.
Sandra Will you help us?
Gerry Of course.

Someone told
write
give
I want you
She said
to do something
for me

9 Choose one of the situations below and write a short dialogue like the one in Exercise 6. Then act it out.

There are plans to build a supermarket where the tennis courts are.

Children are not allowed to use school computers unless a teacher is in the room.

The school library is not open in the afternoon anymore.

They want to fill in the pond in the park to make room for a parking lot.

Skills

Reading and writing

1 **Read about how these people made a difference and answer the questions below.**

ECONOMY and ECOLOGY

Those who speak up can make a difference.

Wangari Maathai. Wangari Maathai (b. 1940) from Kenya won the Nobel Peace Prize in 2004 for her fight for democracy and for the environment. She was the first African woman to win the prize. Maathai founded the Green Belt Movement in Kenya in 1977, which has planted more than 10 million trees. But she went to jail many times because of her fight for the rights of women and because of her work for the environment. In 2002, she won a seat in the Kenyan parliament.

Erin Brockovich. In the early 1990s, Erin Brockovich (b. 1960), a single mother of three, was working for a law firm. While sorting out papers one day, she discovered that many people who lived in and around Hinkley, California, in the 1960s–1980s were very sick. She later found out that there was poison in the water. It came from a gas and electricity company. In 1996, she and lawyer Ed Masry won $333 million for more than 600 people from Hinkley.

Al Gore In 2007, former U.S. vice president Al Gore won a surprising award. It was surprising because what he won was an Oscar, an award normally given to movie stars! He won the Oscar for his 2006 movie, called *An Inconvenient Truth*. This movie tells people about global warming. Since 2000, Al Gore has told millions of people about the effects of global warming. He has also won many awards for his work.

1 What does the Green Belt Movement in Kenya do?
2 Who won the Nobel Peace Prize in 2004?
3 What did Erin Brockovich discover about Hinkley, California?
4 Which "surprising" award did Al Gore win?
5 How many people did Erin Brokovich help win money for?

2 **Summarize what each person did in one sentence.**

Listening

31 **3** **Listen to these students talking about their favorite hero/heroine. Complete the table.**

	Hannah	John	Natasha

Who?	*Mahatma Gandhi*		
Why?			

Speaking

4 **In pairs, talk about your heroes. Then tell the class.**

One of my heroes is ....
I admire him/her because ....
I think it is/was really great, the way she/he ....
I think it's great that she/he ....
She/he usually ....
Once she/he ....
I admire how much .... she/he has.

Writing for your Portfolio

5 **Design a leaflet for something you want to stand up for.**

Make sure you:

- have a good slogan
- say what it is all about
- say what you are planning to do

MAKE RIDING BIKES SAFE!
Say **yes** to a
new bike path!!
Ride to the next meeting and join our
PROTEST RIDE
to the Town Hall!
Saturday, 3:00 p.m.
in front of the school
Keep on riding!

A Song 4 U We shall overcome

32 **6** **Can you name either of the people in the photos? Listen to the song.**

We shall overcome,
We shall overcome,
We shall overcome some day.

Chorus:
Oh deep in my heart,
I do believe,
We shall overcome some day.

We'll walk hand in hand,
We'll walk hand in hand,
We'll walk hand in hand some day.

Chorus

We shall all be free,
We shall all be free,
We shall all be free some day.

Chorus

We are not afraid,
We are not afraid,
We are not afraid today.

Chorus

We are not alone,
We are not alone,
We are not alone today.

Chorus

The whole wide world around,
The whole wide world around,
The whole wide world around some day.

Chorus

We shall overcome,
We shall overcome,
We shall overcome some day.

Chorus

Learn MORE through English

Energy and how to save it

Key words

energy consumption, (energy-saving) lightbulb, average temperature, (powering and lighting) appliances, heat, blackout, increase, tide, gas pump, photovoltaic (PV) cells, wind turbine, insulation, renewable energy, (marine) current, source (of energy)

1 Energy consumption. Read the text.

If you look at North America from space at night, you can see how developed countries light up the world.
Imagine the following situation. It's nine o'clock at night in New York City. Suddenly, there is a blackout in the eastern states of the U.S. Subway trains come to a halt. TV screens go blank, washing machines stop, everything is dark. Blackouts happen because more and more people use more and more energy. In the last 40 years, energy consumption has increased by 250 percent. Scientists think that by the year 2030, energy use will have doubled. And that will cause great problems.

33 **2 How do we use energy at home?**
Guess what people in North America used energy for in 2005. Then listen and check.

1 air-conditioning	About 41%
2 lighting and powering appliances	About 20%
3 heating water	About 26%
4 heating rooms in the house	About 8%

3 Space heating.

The picture on the right shows how energy is lost. In the picture, energy is lost through the windows and walls.

Look at the average temperatures in homes since 1970. What was the increase—20%, 35%, or 50%?

1970	12.6°C
1990	16.9°C
2001	18.9°C

4 **Energy alternatives and saving energy. Read the text.**

Photovoltaic (PV) cells on roof shingles take the sun's energy and generate electricity. Especially in hot countries, solar power will become one of the most important sources of renewable energy in the future.

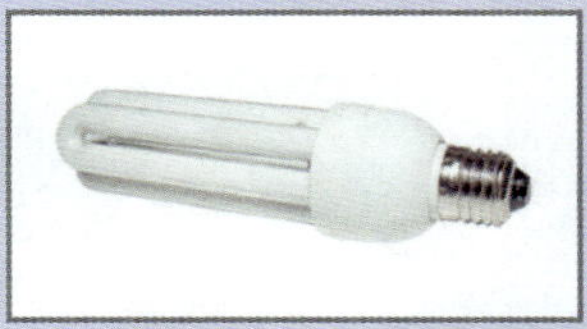

Energy-saving lightbulbs use only a fifth of what traditional bulbs use.

Insulation helps reduce the energy consumption of old houses. When a new house is built, the temperature in the house is higher if the house faces south and if there is a lot of glass that catches the sun.

Wind turbines produce renewable energy, but there is a problem. There have been protests because some people think that they make beautiful landscapes look ugly.

There are currents in the ocean because of the tides. When we use underwater turbines (in much the same way that a wind turbine works), we can make electricity. The advantage is that this form of energy is always there. Work is going on to develop marine current turbines. These could be built in groups under the ocean, like an underwater wind farm.

Think about how you get to school. Many students are driven to school by their parents. You can save energy if you walk or ride your bike to school.

Mini-project Saving energy

5 **Check the Internet or a library for facts about how you can save energy. Design a leaflet, including facts, advice, and illustrations about how to save energy at home or in school.**

UNIT 12 California

1 **Read about California.**

California

Here we come!

"We are in the Joshua Tree National Park in the desert. It's amazing! The shapes of the trees are just incredible. Some look like strange animals!"

"We are in Universal Studios today! It's so cool! There's an earthquake experience and you get attacked by the shark from *Jaws*! We also want to go to the Walk of Fame, where lots of famous actors have a pink star on the sidewalk!"

California
STATE OF CONTRASTS!

by Steven Doyle

Last month, I decided to visit and experience California, one of the most popular and famous states in the U.S. At my hotel, I met David and Emma from the state of Ohio. I asked them why they were here. They said they were on vacation there with their parents, and they told me they were going to the Joshua Tree National Park that day. I saw them later in the evening. They said that the park was amazing. I wanted to know if they planned to visit again. They said they wanted to as there were still so many things to see like Yosemite National Park and San Francisco.

That's the thing about California. It's landscape is diverse, with mountains, deserts, and famous places. Of course, its main attraction must be Hollywood. Thousands of people go there every year to visit the Walk of Fame in Los Angeles and to experience their favorite movies at Universal Studios. I met Jane and Sarah at the hotel who told me their visit to Universal Studios was one of the best days of their lives! So if you want to go to a great place with many different things to see and do, visit the "Sunshine State" of California!

In this unit

You learn
- reported speech 2
- words for physical appearance

and then you can
- justify options
- identify a person

2 **Circle T (True) or F (False) for the sentences below.**

1 California is known as the "Golden State." T / F
2 There are no deserts in California. T / F
3 There is a national park in California. T / F
4 California has a lot different scenery. T / F
5 There is a movie studio you can visit in California. T / F
6 San Francisco and Ohio are in California. T / F

Get talking Justifying opinions

34 **3** **Listen to the sentences and practice saying them.**

1 I love American people. They are so friendly.
2 Universal Studios is so cool! It's fun and interesting.

35 **4** **Match the sentences. Listen and check. Then practice saying them.**

1 The beaches in California are good.
2 The mountains in Yosemite National Park are amazing.
3 San Francisco is great.
4 California is a friendly place.
5 Santa Cruz is a cool city on the coast.

a It's a hilly city and there's always something to do there.
b There's always a big welcome there for you.
c They're really clean and sandy.
d It has some great beaches.
e They're so high.

5 **Make a list of countries and cities you have been to or heard about. Tell a partner about them and justify your opinions.**

London is a bit boring. It's always raining there.

New York City is an exciting city. There's a lot of things to do there.

Language Focus

Vocabulary Physical appearance

hair
body
~~eyes~~
clothes
hair

36 **1 Complete the lists with the words on the left. Listen and check.**

1 gray / blue / brown / green ......eyes......
2 curly / straight / short / long / thin / ....
3 tall / short / thin / slim / well-built / muscular ....
4 casual / elegant / shabby / dressy / dirty / sporty ....
5 blonde / red / gray / brown / white / black / dyed ....

Get talking Identifying a person

2 Work in pairs. Choose a person in the picture. Describe what he or she looks like. Your partner points to the correct person in the picture.

A I'm thinking of a boy. He has red curly hair, his clothes are casual, and he's short and muscular. Who is he?

B This boy here.

Grammar

Reported speech 2

1 Complete the sentences. Then check against the text on page 114.

1 "We want to visit again." → They .... they .... to visit again.
2 "Why are you here?" → I asked them .... they .... here.
3 "Do you plan to visit again?" → I wanted to know .... they .... to visit again.

- When we report someone's words, we often change the verb tense (see sentences 1, 2, and 3).
- When we report a question, we use the same question word (*who/what/why,* etc.) (see sentence 2).
- When we report a *Yes/No* question, we use the word *if* (see sentence 3).
- When we report questions, we don't use *do/does/did* or the question word order (see sentences 2 and 3).

2 Circle the correct form of the verb.

1 Joanne says that she *likes / liked* traveling.
2 Barbara told me that she *is going / was going* to Australia on vacation
3 Our friends said that they *are staying / were staying* at a nice hotel.
4 He said he *doesn't like / didn't like* the beaches in Santa Monica.
5 I said I *am / was* very happy.
6 They tell us that they *love / loved* the sun.
7 She says that she *has / had* no time.
8 You told me you *write / wrote* 10 emails every day.

3 Present or past? Complete the sentences with the correct form of the verb.

1 She told me that her uncle .... on a farm. (live)
2 She says she .... ice cream. (not like)
3 They told us that the weather .... great. (be)
4 Tony says he .... very happy about this. (be)
5 He says he never .... DVDs at home. (watch)
6 They told us that they .... in San Diego. (be)
7 Caroline said that she .... Carl. (love)

4 Complete the sentences. Choose the correct question word.

where ~~why~~ how much if (x3)

1 She said, "Why are you angry?"
She wanted to know ....why..... I was angry.
2 He said, "Do you watch a lot of TV?"
He asked her .... she watched a lot of TV.
3 They asked me, "Are you a student?"
They wanted to know .... I was a student.
4 She asked, "Where's your brother?"
She asked .... my brother was.
5 He said, "Do you like sports?"
He asked .... I liked sports.
6 She asked, "How much are the pink jeans?"
She asked me .... the pink jeans were.

Game

5 **Work in groups of four. Each member of the group needs four strips of paper. Write a different sentence about yourself on each strip of paper. Add your first name. Two of the sentences should be true and two must be false. All four sentences should be in the present tense. Hand out your strips of paper to the other members of the group.**

Sounds right Word stress

37 **6** **Listen to the stress in these words, and then write them in the correct column. Listen again and check.**

A □▢□□

....
....
....
....

B □□▢□

....
....
....
....

politician
information
education
incredible
photographer
European
American
identify

38 **7** **Listen and repeat.**

1 He's an American photographer.
2 I had an incredible education.
3 She's a European politician.
4 I can't identify the information.

Skills

Reading

1 Read the texts. Put the phrases A–D in the correct places.

A This is a place where
B the stars aren't only human
C Don't forget to go on
D a little more contemporary

http://www.latb.com

Los Angeles—some "must do" sightseeing tips for visitors.

Go to Hollywood. Walk along the Walk of Fame to see the stars and their handprints in this famous sidewalk, which includes tributes to Marilyn Monroe and Elvis Presley. The Walk of Fame is on Hollywood Boulevard and Vine Street. (And ☐ ! You can even see the paw prints of Lassie, the movie-star dog from the 1950s!)

Visit Universal Studios. This is one of the most famous film studios in Hollywood. See where and how some of the great movies of all time were made, meet King Kong and Terminator 2. ☐ the Jurassic Ride (which includes a 25m drop at one point).

Go to Venice Beach. Walk along the sidewalks in Venice Beach, watch the skateboarders, or just sit and eat an ice cream. Rent a bicycle and go for a ride. ☐ you might see some famous movie stars!

Spend the day at The California Adventure. This is Disney's latest park, beside Disneyland in Anaheim, but it's ☐ than Disneyland. There are some great rides (such as "California Screaming") but also a lot of cool information about the state of California (its history, its parks, and its people).

Speaking

2 Imagine you have just come back from Los Angeles. Work with a partner. Interview each other about what you did.

1 Where did you go?
2 How long did you stay?
3 Did you have a good time?
4 Did you meet any interesting people?

A Song 4 U California dreaming

39

3 **Listen and complete the song with the words on the left.**

church tell
sky knees
leave walk
cold warm
leaves day

All the leaves are brown,
and the [1]........................ is gray.
I've been for a [2]........................
on a winter's day.
I'd be safe and [3]........................
if I was in L.A.
California dreaming,
on such a winter's [4].........

I stopped into a [5]........................
I passed along the way.
Well, I got down on my [6]................
and I began to pray.
You know, the preacher likes the
[7]........................ ,
he knows I'm gonna stay.
California dreaming,
on such a winter's day.

All the [8]........................are brown,
and the sky is gray.
I've been for a walk
on a winter's day.
If I didn't [9]........................ her,
I could [10]........................ today.
California dreaming,
on such a winter's day.

Writing for your Portfolio

4 **Imagine you are in California. Write a letter to an English-speaking penpal describing what you are doing and the places you have visited. You will find plenty of ideas by looking back through the unit, or find out more things about California on the Internet.**

I am sitting on the beach writing this letter. I can see ...
Yesterday we went to Hollywood, it was ...
On Monday ...
San Francisco is really exciting ...
The best place was ...

Check your progress Units 11 and 12

1 Complete the sentences.

1 Don't be a l _ _ _ _ _ bug.
2 R _ _ _ _ _ _ paper.
3 R _ _ _ your bike.
4 S _ _ _ water.
5 Bring your own b _ _ .

5

2 Complete the sentences.

1 His hair isn't curly. It's s _ _ _ _ _ _ _ .
2 Her clothes are messy and sh _ _ _ _ _
3 He always wears dr _ _ _ _ suits.
4 She has dy _ _ hair.
5 He exercises a lot and is very mu _ _ _ _ _ _.
6 She isn't tall. She is s _ _ _ _ .
7 She always looks nice and e _ _ _ _ _ _ .

7

3 Write sentences using *want someone to do something.*

1 A: ....
B: OK. I'll do the dishes.
2 A: ....
B: OK. Tom will help you with your homework.
3 A: ....
B: OK. Sue will go grocery shopping.

6

4 Complete the sentences with the correct pronoun.

1 Mark: "I'm angry." Mark says .... is angry.
2 Rachel: "We're going on vacation tomorrow." Rachel says .... are going on vacation tomorrow.
3 Sue: "You (pl) are hungry!" Sue says .... are hungry.
4 Tom: "They are going to buy a new car." Tom says .... are going to buy a new car.

4

5 Circle the correct form of the verb.

1 He *told / said* that he didn't like her.
2 They *told / tells* me they were leaving.
3 She *says / tells* that she is happy.
4 He *tells / says* us he is tired.

4

6 Write the sentences in the negative form.

1 I want you to come tomorrow.
....
2 They told me to go.
....
3 We asked them to play on the grass.
....
4 She told us to go home.
....
5 He wants them to leave.
....

10

7 Complete the sentences using indirect speech.

1 She told me her mother .... (be) a teacher.
2 He says he .... (live) near me.
3 They said that they .... (like) ice cream.
4 He tells them he .... (want) some money.

4

8 Rewrite the sentences using indirect speech.

1 "Do you like pizza?" he asked me.
....
2 "Where do you go to school?" she asked him.
....
3 "How much money is there?" he asked me.
....
4 "Are you a teacher?" they asked her.
....
5 "Why are you angry?" he asked them.
....

10

TOTAL 50

My progress so far is ...

great! ☐ good. ☐ poor. ☐

What a waste!

40 **1 Listen and then answer the questions about plastic.**

1 What is the problem with plastic?
2 How long will plastic stay in a landfill?
3 Why don't companies want to buy plastic for recycling?
4 What is *Mater-Bi* made of?
5 What is different about *Mater-Bi*?

Do you know?

A lot of the waste produced in the Western world is plastic. Most of the food and drinks we buy in supermarkets are packed in plastic, and in some countries plastic makes up 20 percent of all waste. All of the electronic and electrical appliances we use (such as fridges, cell phones, and laptops) are made of plastic. Plastic is very difficult to get rid of.

2 Read the text and complete the chart.

An average cell phone has a lifespan of five years. However, people usually only use a cell phone for about 18 months before they get a new one.

In the U.S., about 130 million cell phones are "retired" each year. That equals about 65,000 tons of electronic garbage. Cell phones contain some dangerous materials. They need to be disposed of in a safe way.

Thankfully, more and more organizations will help you recycle cell phones. Some take your phones for charity. Others may even give you money for a used cell phone.

Phones for recycling
There are some valuable materials in mobile phones such as gold, silver, and copper. The metals are taken out and reused in jewelry, copper pipes, or new cell phones. The plastic can be reused in traffic cones or printer cartridges.

Phones for reuse and repair
Handsets are very expensive and in some countries in Africa and Eastern Europe, people cannot afford them. Phones are sent to these countries and they are given or resold cheaply.

Reseach on the Internet to see which cell phone recycling programs are available where you live.

How long do people usually use a cell phone?
1...

How many cell phones are "retired" in the U.S. every year?
2...

How do cell phones need to be disposed of?
3...

How are phones recycled?
4...

What happens to cell phones that are reused?
5...

3 Over 2 U! In pairs, plan a recycling program for your class or school.

MORE! Now you can watch Episode 6 of *The School Magazine*! DVD

Learn MORE about Culture

The sound of California

One of the hottest states in the U.S. has also been providing some of the hottest pop and rock music for over half a century. Here are some of the most famous artists from the Sunshine State.

The 1960s

Forget the Beatles and the Rolling Stones! Many critics will tell you that the most influential band in rock history is, in fact, The Beach Boys. The band was started in 1961 in Hawthorne, California, by brothers Brian, Carl, and Denis Wilson, with their cousin Mike Love and friend Alan Jardine.

Their early songs were about being young in California, and talked of things like the sun, beaches, cars (*Fun, Fun, Fun,* and *Little Deuce Coupe*) and surfing (*Surfin' Safari,* and *Surfin' USA*). But as the band got older, their songs became more sophisticated.

During the mid-1960s the band produced their greatest album, *Pet Sounds,* and the single *Good Vibrations*, which is considered by many people as the greatest rock song of all time.

The 1970s

The Eagles were formed in the early 1970s in Los Angeles. Over the next 10 years, they became the best-selling American band of all time with five number one singles and four number one albums. Their *Greatest Hits* album has sold more copies worldwide than any other album except Michael Jackson's *Thriller*.

They are famous for their easy-going, country-style rock made popular by songs such as *Take It Easy, Lying Eyes, Life in the Fast Lane,* and, of course, *Hotel California*.

The band broke up in 1980 but got back together again in 1994 for a series of successful shows around the world. They have also started to record new music to introduce a new generation of fans to the sound of southern California.

The new millennium

In 2006, the Red Hot Chili Peppers showed that they really are the biggest Californian band on the planet when their new CD, *Stadium Arcadium*, went straight into the charts at number one in 27 countries around the world. The band started in 1983 when former Fairfax High School students, Michael "Flea" Balzary (bass), Anthony Kiedis (vocals), Jack Irons (drums), and Hillel Slovak (guitar) got together.

They first played under the name Tony Flow and the Miraculously Majestic Masters of Mayhem. Less than a year later, they were really popular on the Los Angeles rock scene and signed a deal with EMI. Since then, they have released nine studio albums and played to millions of fans all over the world.

With their mixture of alternative rock, punk, rap, funk, and heavy metal, the Red Hot Chili Peppers have created what many people consider to be the sound of modern California.

And the future? These days there are plenty of new up-and-coming bands from California–bands such as Black Rebel Motorcycle Club, The Warlocks, and Scarling. You haven't heard of them yet but wait a few years. And even if none of these bands make it big, you can be sure that it won't be long before the next big band from California hits the music world.

For MORE! Go to www.more-online.com/american and take a quiz on this text.

Herbert Puchta & Jeff Stranks
G. Gerngross C. Holzmann P. Lewis-Jones

American MORE! 3B

COMBO Workbook

HELBLING LANGUAGES
CAMBRIDGE UNIVERSITY PRESS
editora ática

CONTENTS

UNIT 7 I didn't use to like them

17

1 Complete the dialogue using the phrases below. Then listen and check.

I used to listen to *I also used to collect* *I used to like them a lot*
the Stones used to be my favorite

Mandy What are you listening to?
Tony One of my old Rolling Stones albums. [1] ....
Mandy So did I. Actually I still like them. I even have their album *Forty Licks*.
Tony So do I!
Mandy Do you listen to a lot of old bands?
Tony Not really, but [2]... band. [3].. the soundtracks of Disney movies. I loved *The Lion King* and *Toy Story*.
Mandy Yeah, I can understand that! [4].. the soundtrack of *The Little Mermaid* all the time!
Tony Yeah. That was a good one.

2 Answer the questions.

1 What is Tony listening to?
2 Who has the album *Forty Licks* ?
4 What did Tony use to collect when he was a kid?
5 What did Mandy use to listen to?

3 Write sentences about what they used to like.

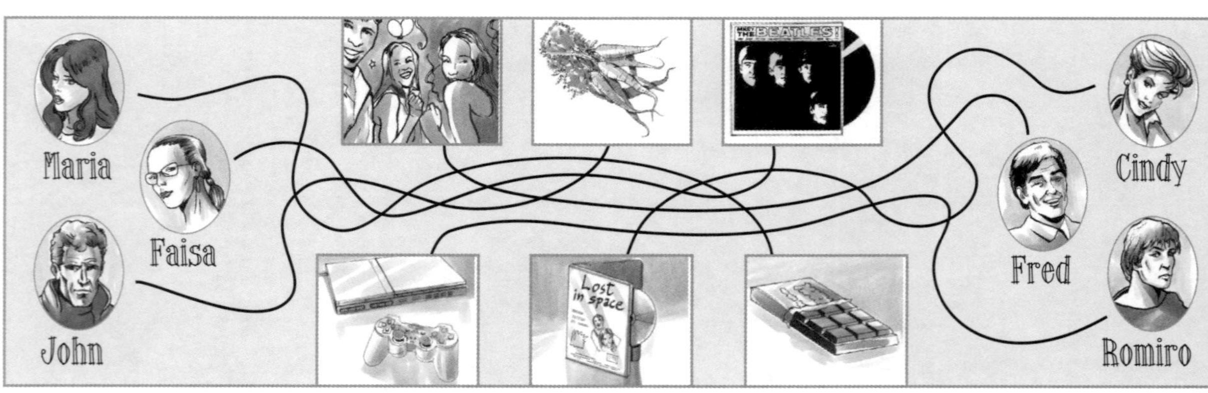

1 Maria ....
2 Faisa ....
3 John ....
4 Cindy ....
5 Fred ....
6 Romiro ....

Language Focus

Vocabulary Music

1 Write the words for the musical styles.

1 lsebu ....blues........
2 cork ....
3 kolf ....
4 ppo ....
5 lacsacils ....
6 eindi ....
7 rapoe ....
8 mtela veayh ....

2 Match the singers and bands with six of the musical styles above.

a

b

c

d

e

f

Agreeing and disagreeing

3 Complete the dialogue with the phrases below.

Neither have I   used to like   So did I   So am I
I don't   I didn't like it   ~~did you use to like~~

Joanna What kind of music[1] *did you use to like*, Sandra?
Sandra When I was in elementary school I [2]................ Boys II Men.
Joanna [3]................! I thought they were great. I still listen to them sometimes.
Sandra Really? [4]................ . I like rock music now.
Joanna Have you heard Incubus's latest CD?
Sandra Yes, but [5]................
Joanna Didn't you? I agree it wasn't as good as the first one, but I'm still going to their concert.
Sandra [6]................, but I don't have my ticket yet.
Joanna [7]................ . Let's hope they come soon!

18 **4 Listen and check.**

Grammar

used to

1 Put the words in the correct order.

1 ice cream / day. / to / eat / lemon / used / every / I

....

2 used / earn / to / lawns / I / to / money. / some / mow

....

3 cars. / used / I / wash / to

....

4 lemon / used / money. / I / buy / to / the / myself / with / ice cream

....

5 at / me. / to / used / people / laugh

....

6 to / used / "Lemony." / call / me / they

....

2 Complete with the phrases below.

used to listen to   used to take   didn't use to drink   didn't use to watch

1 When I was younger, I .... milk.
2 My brother and I .... our grandfather's stories.
3 Our mother .... us to the theater once a week.
4 We .... as much TV as we do today.

3 Write sentences about Karen.

	2001	Now
1 play tennis	no	yes
2 eat salad	no	yes
3 eat popcorn	yes	no
4 drink soda	yes	no
5 watch TV all night	yes	no
6 go for walks	no	yes
7 go to bed late	yes	no

1 *She didn't use to play tennis.*
2 ....
3 ....
4 ....
5 ....
6 ....
7 ....

4 Write sentences about Mr. Trimble.

1 *He used to have long hair.*
2 ....
3 ....
4 ....
5 ....
6 ....

so do I / neither do I

5 Complete with the phrases below

So will I. So did I. So can I. So have I.
~~Neither do I~~. Neither did I. Neither can I. Neither have I.

1 **A** I don't like punk music.
B *Neither do I.*

2 **A** I can't help Helen with all her problems.
B ....

3 **A** I'll talk to the teacher about this.
B ....

4 **A** We didn't really enjoy the food.
B ....

5 **A** I have the latest computer game.
B ....

6 **A** I can help out in the kitchen.
B ....

7 **A** We haven't booked our vacation yet.
B ....

8 **A** I ran the last mile in less than 10 minutes.
B ....

6 Complete the replies

1 **A** We didn't see the play.
B *Neither did I.*

2 **A** I can't think of a birthday present for Dad.
B .... I.

3 **A** I'm reading the latest *Twilight* book.
B .... I.

4 **A** We've talked to our parents about the trip.
B .... I.

5 **A** I'll help Sarah with her packing.
B .... I.

6 **A** We didn't go to Arizona.
B .... I.

7 **A** I won't eat any dessert.
B .... I.

8 **A** I can't meet him on Saturday.
B .... I.

7 Complete the poem with the phrases below

so can I neither have I ~~neither can I~~ so will I so am I so do I

Can you fly?

You can't fly (and neither can I).
But you can try (and ....).
You see the sky (and ....).
You'll land nearby (and ....).
You haven't gone high (and ....).
You're going to cry (and ....).

Grammar

8 Put the lines of the dialogue in the correct order.

A No. I used to like it, but now I think it's awful. ☐
A What kind of music do you like? 1
A Me too. I used to like pop music, but not anymore. ☐
B I really like rock music. ☐
B You're crazy! Indie's great. I didn't use to like it, but now I listen to it every day. ☐
B Oh? I still like pop, but rock's my favorite. Do you like indie music? ☐

Sounds right Elision

19 **9 Listen and repeat.**

1 I used to play tennis.
2 Some cats eat grass.
3 They used to drink coffee.
4 I like rock music and folk music.

Skills

Listening

20 **1 Listen to Tania and Jack. Circle the correct answer: a, b, or c.**

1 What is the name of the music show they watched?
a Top of the Pops **b** Hot Pops **c** Hip-hop

2 Who did not like the music on the show?
a Only Jack **b** Only Tania **c** Jack and Tania

3 What is Jack's favorite kind of music?
a Pop **b** Rock **c** Hip-hop

4 What kind of music does Tania like?
a Rock and classical **b** Pop and classical **c** Rock and pop

5 Why doesn't Tania download music?
a She likes having the CD. **b** She doesn't have a computer. **c** Her computer is broken.

Reading

2 **Read the interview and match the questions below with the answers.**

On the spot

this week Johnny Y from **Bestboyz** talks about music

- ☐ The Rolling Stones. I know they're an old band, but I think they're really cool. And they've written some great tunes. I saw them play last year. They were incredible.
- ☐ I like songs with a good tune that you can sing along to. I don't care so much about the lyrics.
- ☐ "I Believe I Can Fly" by R. Kelly. That song makes me feel like I can do anything if I put my mind to it.
- ☐ "Yesterday," by the Beatles. I like most of their songs, but that one is just awful! Maybe it's because I've heard it too many times.
- ☐ Not really, but if the song's good, then maybe I'll go on the dance floor for a few minutes.
- ☐ Anywhere, but I really enjoy listening to music in my car, especially if I'm in a traffic jam. It helps me relax.
- ☐ I buy CDs from my local music store. I usually buy two or more a week.

1 What well-known song do you dislike the most?
2 Do you like dancing?
3 Where do you get your music?
4 What's your favorite band?
5 Which song is special to you?
6 Where do you like listening to music?
7 What's the most important thing in a song for you?

Writing for your Portfolio

3 **Choose five of the questions in Exercise 2. Write your answers to them.**

....

....

....

....

....

UNIT 8 Natural disasters

1 Read the article about a week of terrible fires in California.

Fire!

Forest fires have become very common in southern California during the past decade. A big wake-up call about the dangers of forest fires in California came in 2003, when several forest fires started in the southern part of the state. For a week firefighters tried to fight the flames, but they did not have a chance against them. More than 20 people were killed and many houses were destroyed.

On October 31, the people living in the Lake View Estates neighborhood realized that the flames were getting very close. They saw that the firefighters were helpless as the wind blew the flames in their direction. The lucky ones grabbed a few important things, rushed to their cars, and drove away before the flames got too close.

One family, however, waited too long. When they tried to drive to a nearby reservoir, they were trapped in the flames and died in their car. Another couple who also waited too long and could not get out of the Lake View Estates did not die. They were lucky. When the flames destroyed their house, they dived into their swimming pool and survived.

The fires burned for more than a week and then it got colder, fog rolled in from the ocean, and the flames died down.

Experts say that there have been forest fires for thousands of years. When it is very dry in California and a hot wind blows out of the desert, the smallest ember may be enough to start a terrible fire.

2 Answer the questions.

1 For how long did the firefighters fight the flames?
2 How many houses were destroyed?
3 How many people died?
4 What did most people do when the flames came close?
5 How did a couple survive who waited too long to get away?
6 Was this fire in October 2003 the first fire in this area?

Language Focus

Vocabulary Catastrophes

1 Complete the sentences with the words below.

earthquake hit flames rescue rushed erupted trapped traveled

1 The tsunami quickly .... toward the coast of India.
2 A boy was .... under a collapsed house.
3 A .... dog found the man after six days.
4 The coast was .... by a huge wave that was 10 meters high.
5 The .... that hit the island measured 6.9 on the Richter scale.
6 The volcano .... on May 16.
7 The wind blew the .... in the direction of the house.
8 When the flames came closer the people .... to their cars.

2 Match the pictures with the sentences from Exercise 1.

Explaining things in simpler words

3 Work in pairs. Look at the example dialogue and make up new dialogues using the words below.

cabbage factory horse trailer estate

A What's an avalanche?
B An avalanche?
A Yes.
B It's a large mass of snow and ice that falls down the side of a mountain.
A Thanks.

Grammar

too / not ... enough

1 **Rewrite the sentences so they mean the same thing. Use *not... enough* or *too*.**

1 It's too cold to go swimming.
.... (warm)
2 He's not old enough to be on our team.
.... (young)
3 I'm too poor to buy a car like that.
.... (rich)
4 He's not tall enough to get the apple.
.... (small)
5 There isn't enough light in here. Let's go!
It's .... (dark)

2 **Circle the correct option to complete the sentences.**

1 The volume is *too loud / not loud enough*. I can't hear anything.
2 This bag is *too heavy / not heavy enough*. I can't lift it.
3 You must be 18 or older to see this movie. You're *too old / not old enough*.
4 I got 100% on the test. It was *too difficult / not difficult enough*.
5 She's *too smart / not smart enough* to be a doctor.
6 We're *too tired / not tired enough* to study any more.
7 The movie was *too long / not long enough*. It was pretty boring.
8 Your face is *too clean / not clean enough*. Go and wash it again.

Past passive

3 **Read the description and underline the examples of the simple past passive.**

The World Series is the baseball championship games that take place every year in North America. It started in 1903 and has been played just about every year since.

One of the most famous World Series was played between the New York Yankees and the Pittsburgh Pirates. The year was 1960 and the Yankees were expected to come out on on top.

The Yankees, a team that had dominated the sport for years, were forced into a tough position. After six games and another six innings, the two teams were tied.

The Pirates were up at bat. Their lead hitter, Bill Mazeroski, hit a homerun. For the first time in the history of the World Series, a home run ended a final game.

That year the World Series was won by the Pirates, but the Yankees would come back again to win the series in 1961 and a dozen or so more times since.

4 **Use the names below to complete the famous people quiz.**

Roger Federer	J.K. Rowling	Marie Curie
Leonardo da Vinci	James Cameron	Ernő Rubik
Paul McCartney	Alexander Graham Bell	

The famous people quiz

1 Wimbledon 2005 was won by

....

2 *Titanic* was directed by

....

3 *Harry Potter* was written by

....

4 Radium was discovered by

....

5 The telephone was invented by

....

6 The first rubik's cube was made by

....

7 "Yesterday" was sung by

....

8 The *Mona Lisa* was painted by

....

5 **Write sentences for the pictures.**

1 worm / eat / bird
The worm was eaten by the bird.

2 boy / hit / ball
....
....

3 race / win / a girl
....
....

4 TV show / make / children
....
....

5 house / destroy / earthquake
....
....

6 boy / chase / dog
....
....

7 plane / delay / fog
....
....

8 vase / break / cat
....
....

6 **Make the active sentences passive and the passive sentences active.**

1 John's uncle took him to the theater yesterday.
John was taken to the theater by his uncle yesterday.

2 Our house was built 10 years ago by my uncle.
....

3 Millions of emails were sent out within two hours by the computer.
....

4 My older brother bought this camera for me.
....

Grammar

7 **Write dialogues similar to the one below.**

1	2	3
Romeo and Juliet / write / William Shakespeare / 1597	Guggenheim / design / Frank Lloyd Wright / 1959	*Help* / release / the Beatles /1965
A *When was Romeo and Juliet written?*	**A**	**A** ....
B *In 1597.*	**B**	**B** ....
A *Who was it written by?*	**A**	**A** ....
B *William Shakespeare.*	**B**	**B** ....

Sounds right Silent letters

21 **8** **Listen and repeat. Pay attention to the underlined silent letters.**

1 I didn't know the answer to the last question on the test.
2 It took half a day for the baby calf to be born on the farm yesterday.
3 I knelt down on my knees to pick up my baseball.

Skills

Listening

22 **1** **Listen to the radio show. Write down the things Tom Newman chooses.**

1 CD ....
2 book ....
3 movie ....
4 special thing ....

23 **2** **Listen again and match the items in Exercise 1 with his reasons for taking them.**

1 It makes me feel happy.
2 It's really interesting.
3 It has a lot of practical advice on how to survive.
4 It makes me feel like I'm home.

Reading

3 Read the article. Then answer the questions.

A week on a desert island

Naseli and Lisa Nona were in a boat on their way from Badu Island to a birthday party on Thursday Island. With them were their four children, Ellis (15), Stephen (12), Norita (10), and three-year-old Pete. The journey normally takes two hours. The family was about halfway between Badu and Thursday Island when the motor of their boat stopped. Then the weather turned really bad, and suddenly the boat was overturned by the strong wind.

The children and their parents stayed in the water near their boat for awhile, but then Ellis, Stephen, and Norita were told by their parents to swim to the nearest island. The three children swam for about three hours before they reached a little rock. They climbed onto the rock and hoped for a boat to come and rescue them. But nobody came and so the children had to stay on the rock for three days and nights without water or food. Then the sisters were persuaded by Stephen to swim to another island. "We must try to get there," he said, "or we'll die!"

The children were lucky. They were not attacked by sharks, and when they reached the island, they found oysters, plums, and coconuts. Finally, six days later, they were found on the island by their uncle.

1 Where was the family when their boat was hit by bad weather?
2 What other problem was there and what happened?
3 Why didn't the children stay with their parents?
4 Where did they stay for three days and why did they leave?
5 Who were the children found by?
6 How did they survive on the desert island?

Writing for your Portfolio

4 Imagine you are going to stay on a desert island for a month. Write what you are going to take.

First of all I want to take a book with me. The book I'd take is … because …
I love music and that is why I'd take … with me. It's my favorite album.
Of course I also want to take …
I think I'm going to need … and …
Finally, I wouldn't go to the island without … because …

UNIT 9 If I had the money,...

24 **1 Read the dialogue and cross out the sentences that do not belong.**

Kathy If I had my flash drive with me, we could save your file on it.
Rick Umh! ~~There was an advertisement with a flying elephant~~. That doesn't really help me now, does it?
Kathy It's all your fault. If you listened to me sometimes, we wouldn't have these problems!
Rick I listened alright. You're the one with the flash drive. I also listen to the radio.
Kathy OK, so I forgot it. But it's for your homework!
Rick If there were disks somewhere, I'd save it on them.
Kathy But it's a very large file.
Rick I know, but if I split it into two, it would go on two disks.
Kathy What about Mr. Trimble? He's just bought a new jacket. I'm sure he would help if we asked him nicely.
Rick If I were you, I'd think of someone else. He's not talking to me.
Kathy Why not?
Rick What time is it? I lost his flash drive.

2 Tom needs some extra money. Write advice using *if I were you...*

Tom I need some extra money.
Girl 1 If I were you, I wouldn't spend so much.
2 ....
3 ....
4 ....

Language Focus

Vocabulary Computer words

1 Write the words.

Talking about people

2 Complete the dialogues with the words below.

everyone someone no one ~~anyone~~ anyone

1 **A** I'm looking for Cathy Black. Does [1]*anyone* in here know her?
B No, [2]........................ knows her. She's probably new.

2 **A** OK, [3]........................ listen to me please.
B Yes, Mr. Collins.
A [4]........................ has taken my pen. Who was it?

3 **A** I'm looking for Miss Wayne.
B OK. Has [5]........................ seen Miss Wayne? No? Sorry, she's not here right now.

25 **3 Listen and check.**

4 Finish the sentences.

1 I know a boy/girl who ....
2 On the weekend, almost everyone ....
3 Among my friends, no one ....
4 On my team, there is someone who ....
5 In the evening, no one ....
6 In my family, everyone ....
7 In my class, there is no one who ....

Grammar

Second conditional

1 Match the sentence halves.

1 If I had enough money, *b*
2 If my brother had a problem,
3 If I found some money on the sidewalk,
4 If you studied more,
5 If I were president,
6 If my mother didn't work so hard,
7 If I were 18,
8 If you knew the answer,

a you'd get better grades.
b I'd buy a new computer.
c I'd go and live in my own apartment.
d would you tell me?
e she wouldn't be tired in the evening.
f I'd take it to the police station.
g I'd change a lot of things.
h I'd help him.

2 Put the verb in parentheses into the correct form.

1 If my father *were* (be) here, I *would be* (be) very happy.
2 If she .... (not live) in Ohio, I .... (see) her more often.
3 If I .... (have) a dictionary, I .... (look) this word up.
4 If my computer .... (not be) broken, I .... (write) some emails.
5 If your mother .... (here), she .... (not let) you do that!
6 The teacher .... (be) angry if she .... (know).
7 He .... (hear) you if you .... (shout).
8 What .... you .... (do) if your parents .... (give) you a lot of money?

3 Write the sentences.

1 I don't like Sally. I don't talk to her.
If I liked Sally, I'd talk to her.
2 He doesn't have a computer. I don't send him emails.
If ....
3 She's sick. She isn't at school.
If ....
4 I like you. I help you with your homework.
If ....
5 They're on vacation. They aren't here today.
If ....
6 My modem is broken. I can't surf the Internet.
If ....
7 I don't have a big house. I don't invite my friends to stay.
If ....
8 Tom doesn't enjoy traveling. He doesn't go abroad.
If ....

If I were you Giving advice

4 **Create sentences using the phrases below.**

~~go home~~ see a doctor feed it not wear it play a different sport

1 *If I were you, I'd go home.*

2 If ....

3 If ....

4 If ....

5 If ....

Indefinite pronouns Everyone, someone, no one, anyone

5 **Circle the correct option: *everyone, someone, no one,* or *anyone.***

1 It was a sad movie. *Everyone* / *Anyone* cried.
2 Would you like *no one* / *someone* to come to the doctor with you?
3 It's raining, so *anyone* / *no one* is on the beach.
4 The room was empty. There was *no one* / *anyone* in it.
5 It was a great party. *Everyone* / *Anyone* enjoyed themselves.
6 Does *anyone* / *everyone* want to play tennis tomorrow?
7 The theater was full. Just about *everyone* / *anyone* wanted to see the movie.
8 John, there's *someone* / *no one* here who wants to see you.

6 **Complete with the correct indefinite pronoun.**

1 *Everyone* looked for my pen, but they couldn't find it.
2 I don't know .... who understands computers.
3 I know .... who can help me with my math homework.
4 This is so easy that .... can do it!
5 The new theme park is great. .... wants to go.
6 John knows, Ally knows, you know—........................ knows!
7 Look! There's .... in the park.
8 The party was awful. .... enjoyed it.

Grammar

7 Put the dialogue in the correct order.

A	OK. But I mean where would you go?	☐
A	And what would you do in New York City?	☐
A	What would you do if you won a trip to the U.S.?	1
A	And where would you go after New York City?	☐
A	What's that? I've never heard of it.	☐
B	I'd come home. New York City's the only place I'd want to see!	☐
B	New York City. I've always wanted to go there.	☐
B	A lot of things. I'd go to Yankee Stadium, for sure.	☐
B	Well, first, I would jump up and down because I would be very happy!	☐
B	It's a baseball stadium. The New York Yankees play there. I'd want to watch a game there.	☐

Sounds right /d/

26 **8 Listen and circle the words you hear.**

1 *I go / I'd go* home.
2 *They run / They'd run* away.
3 *You laugh / You'd laugh* at me!
5 *I like / I'd like* a nice, hot shower.
4 *We go / We'd go* to Florida.
6 *I say / I'd say* the same thing.

Skills

Listening

27 **1 Listen to the radio show and circle the correct answer: a, b, or c.**

1 Jenny saw John, her best friend, ...
a at the park.
b at the theater.
c at school.

2 She noticed that John was ...
a a little nervous.
b very tired.
c sick.

3 When John left, ...
a he didn't say anything to Jenny.
b he said goodbye.
c he was crying.

4 Sandra was studying ...
a biology.
b history.
c math.

5 Donald's friend is stealing ...
a from his friends.
b from a store.
c from his mother's purse.

6 After Donald's phone call, the host plays a song by ...
a the Eagles.
b Metallica.
c the Rolling Stones.

Reading

2 **Read the chat page and answer the questions..**

Last week, I asked:
"Are computers really useful?"
My answer was: "No!" Here's what some of my readers wrote.

BILLY JAMESON'S CHAT PAGE

AUREL BIGGS (16)
I think you're right, Billy. I've got a desktop at home, but it's not that important to me. I use my cell phone a lot more than my computer. I send emails and text messages to all my friends with my cell phone, so why should I sit down at a computer? If I didn't have a computer, I wouldn't miss it much.

ANTONIO HOPWOOD (14)
I'd be totally lost if I didn't have my computer. Our family recently moved, so I use the Internet all the time to find out about things back home, email my friends and learn about my new city. It's good for relaxing too. I don't have a lot of friends to hang out with yet, so I play a lot of computer games after school. Computers are great, Billy, so don't knock them!

DAV VASUDEVA (15)
Sorry, Billy, but you're wrong! Computers are absolutely necessary—at home, at school, everywhere. Can you imagine if banks and offices didn't have computers? Or libraries? You only talked about computers at home, but if you thought about it a little more, you'd see that that's only a small part of the picture. And even at home I can't imagine trying to do school projects without my computer and the Internet!!!

1 Who asked the question "Are computers really useful?" *Billy Jameson*
2 Two readers think computers are good things. Which two readers? ....
3 Which reader has recently moved? ....
4 Who uses a computer to "talk" to friends? ....
5 Who uses a cell phone to "talk" to friends? ....
6 Who says Billy should think more? ....

Writing for your Portfolio

3 **Write your answer to the question: "Are computers really useful?"**

....
....
....
....
....

UNIT 10 Into the wilderness

1 Read the description of a tour to the Okavango Delta in Botswana.

Africa | Botswana

Classic Botswana

What is the Okavango Delta?

It is one of the world's most famous areas of wilderness. The delta is formed by thousands of channels of crystal clear water from the Okavango River. There are a lot of small islands and larger dry open areas with bush and a lot of trees. The Okavango is home to more than 400 different kinds of birds and large herds of buffalo, antelopes, and elephants. You will also find crocodiles, hippos, cheetahs, leopards, lions, and different kinds of monkeys.

What do you do at your camp?

You get up at six o'clock and have a large breakfast. Then, at six thirty, the first drive of the day starts. This lasts until 10:00 or 11:00. When you stay in a camp in one of the large, dry areas you go on game drives in a four-wheel vehicle. When you stay in a water camp you either go by boat or in a type of canoe known as a "mokoro." There are only seats for two people in a mokoro. A guide uses a long pole to push the canoe along.

When you come back to the camp, lunch is waiting for you. Then you can rest or relax until five o'clock. At five the second drive of the day takes place and part of it is in darkness. The guides use a spotlight to look for animals.

When you come back at about nine or ten in the evening, dinner is waiting for you. Afterward you may have a chat round the campfire. When you go to bed, a guide will go with you to your cabin or tent as there may be wild animals such as elephants or lions around.

2 Answer the questions.

1 What kind of animals can you see?
2 What does the Okavango Delta look like?
3 Where can you sleep at a camp?
4 When does the morning drive start?
5 How many hours does the morning drive last?
6 What is a mokoro?
7 When will you come back from the afternoon drive?
8 Why will a guide go with you when you go to bed?

Language Focus

Vocabulary Vacation words

1 Look at the pictures. Complete the phrases with the words and match them to the pictures.

rent learn arrive ~~do~~ go show visit take have stay in

1 ....do.......... some sightseeing
2 .... a car
3 .... your passport
4 .... a plane
5 .... to scuba dive
6 .... on safari
7 .... at a campsite
8 .... a hotel
9 .... a museum
10 .... breakfast

Talking about vacation plans

2 Complete the dialogue with the words below.

interested do going weeks take a lot of animals plans

A Do you have any [1]........................ for your vacation yet?
B Yes, I'm [2]........................ to Botswana with my parents.
A What are you going to [3]........................ there?
B My mom and dad are [4]........................ in wildlife.
A What kind of [5]........................ can you see there?
B Elephants, hippos, giraffes, lions, and [6]........................ others.
A How many [7]........................ will you be away?
B Two.
A Are you going to [8]........................ any photos?
B Of course I am.

Grammar

Making deductions

1 Write the sentences under the pictures.

They must be twins.	They can't be twins.	He can't be a tourist.
He must be a tourist.	It must be San Francisco.	It can't be San Francisco.

1 ....

2 ....

3 ....

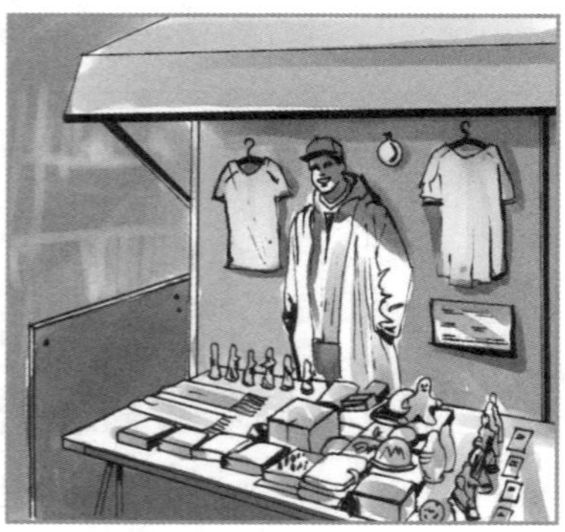

4 ....

5 ....

6 ....

2 Circle the correct option.

1 James' goldfish died last week. He *can't* / *must* be very sad.
2 Erica swims for an hour every day. She *can't* / *must* be in great shape.
3 Lucy and William are painting their apartment. They *can't* / *must* be very busy.
4 You slept until 11:00 this morning. You *can't* / *must* be tired.
5 He never listens to music. He *can't* / *must* know a lot of songs.
6 She has a dog, a cat, and a hamster. She *can't* / *must* love animals.
7 John got the best grade on the math test. His parents *can't* / *must* be pleased.
8 Your favorite team is winning everything. You *can't* / *must* be happy.

3 Think about six people. Write a sentence about each of them, making deductions.

My mother *is working late in the office. She must be very busy.*
My best friend ....
Our English teacher ....
People in my town ....
People in New York City ....

Causative *have*

4 **Mark the sentences N (normal passive) or C (causative passive).**

1 I've had my hair cut. Do you like it? ......
2 Yesterday the trees in our yard were cut down. ......
3 A lot of cars were sold in the first half of last year. ......
4 They had a swimming pool built. ......
5 Their new house was finished last week. ......
6 My dad's car was repaired by one of his friends. ......

5 **Rewrite the sentences to include the causative *have*.**

1 The teacher graded our homework.
We had our homework ....
2 The new stylist is going to do my hair.
I'm going to ....
3 A gardener cut our trees.
We had ....
4 My uncle fixed my bike.
I had my ....

Infinitives of purpose

6 **Join the sentences together. Use *to* and *because*.**

1 Tom bought a new car. He wants to go on vacation with it.
Tom bought a new car to go on vacation.
/ Tom bought a new car because he wants to go on vacation with it.
2 My dad took out his credit card. He wanted to pay.
3 Mary called me. She wanted to tell me something.
4 I hope you have some time. I want you to help me with my homework.
5 She went into the kitchen. She wanted to make herself a sandwich.
6 I took some money with me. I wanted to buy myself an ice-cream cone.

7 **Complete the sentences.**

1 Mario stayed up late to
....
....

2 Kate went to bed at eight
because ....
....

3 Terry is saving money to
....
....

Grammar

8 **Put the sentences in the correct places to complete the dialogue.**

Was it expensive there?
They let my sister have her hair dyed.
Where did you have it done?
I want to have my hair dyed, too.
I had it cut on Saturday.

Betty Have you had your hair cut?
Helen Yes. [1] ....
Betty It looks really good!
Helen Thanks. I like it a lot, too.
Betty [2] ....
Helen At Julio's. You know, the new salon in town.
Betty Oh, I know. [3] ....
Helen Not really. I'm going back next week.
Betty Why?
Helen [4] ....
Betty Wow. Will your parents let you?
Helen Sure. Why not? [5] ....

Sounds right Question intonation

28 **9** **Listen and repeat.**

1 What time is it? Is it three o'clock?
2 How old is he? Is he 16?
3 Who did that? Was it you?
4 Where are you going? Are you going to school?

Skills

Listening

29 **1** **Listen to the conversation. Circle T (True) or F (False).**

1 Oliver thinks there are leopard skins in the store window. T / F
2 They are just imitations. T / F
3 The store sells a lot of animal products. T / F
4 The store doesn't sell anything made of wood. T / F
5 Leopards are in danger. T / F
6 Tourists never buy wildlife souvenirs in Africa. T / F
7 Tourists are fined more than $2 million for bringing illegal souvenirs into the U.S. T / F
8 It is illegal to bring things made from ivory into the U.S. T / F

Reading

2 **Read the Fact File and circle the correct answers.**

LEOPARD FACT FILE

- **Leopards are the smallest of the great cats.** They are smaller than lions, tigers, and jaguars. However, the male leopard can be 50% bigger than the female.
- **Leopards can hear five times better than humans.** They can hear sounds that we can't hear at all!
- **Leopards like to climb trees and sleep on the branches.**
- **Leopards like water and they're strong swimmers.** They can run very fast (58 kilometers an hour), jump 6 meters forward, and 3 meters straight up.
- **Leopards are extremely strong.** A leopard can climb as high as 15 meters up a tree holding a dead animal in its mouth, even one that's bigger and heavier than itself! They hide their food up in the trees so that lions or hyenas can't get it. Then they can return later and eat more.
- **Leopards can also be completely black because of a condition called "melanism."** Black leopards are often called panthers, but they belong to exactly the same family as spotted leopards. In fact, panthers are spotted, but because they are black you can't see the spots.
- **The leopard uses its spots for camouflage.** They let a leopard get close to its prey and attack by surprise. Like human fingerprints, all leopards' spots are different.
- **Leopards are not fussy.** They will eat anything they can get, including monkeys, rats, frogs, fish, wild pigs, and birds. Unlike lions, which only hunt at night, leopards always hunt during the day.

1 Which of these is not a "great" cat?
a panther **b** tiger **c** ocelot **d** leopard

2 Where do leopards usually sleep?
a on the ground **b** in caves **c** by rivers **d** in trees

3 How high can a leopard jump?
a 3m **b** 6m **c** 15m **d** 58m

4 What does melanism do to a panther?
a makes it lose its spots **b** turns it black **c** makes it hungry

5 How are leopards and lions similar?
a They hunt at night. **b** They are "great" cats. **c** They are the same size.

Writing for your Portfolio

3 **Choose another animal and write a fact file about it. Use the Fact File above as a model.**

....

....

....

....

UNIT 11 He told us not to worry

30 **1 Complete the dialogue with the words below. Then listen and check.**

stick to the rules *organize a protest* *should talk* *promise* *last year* *unfair*

Karen Did you hear about the prom?
Julian No, what about it?
Karen The principal says we aren't allowed to have one.
Julian But that's [1] .... There's always been one. How do you know he said that?
Karen The principal asked Mr. Jenkins to tell all the students at the assembly.
Julian Did Mr. Jenkins say why we aren't allowed to have a prom?
Karen Yes, he said that some boys broke a window [2] ....
Julian What's that got to do with us?
Karen He said students had to behave and [3] .... If they don't, they can't have a prom.
Julian Listen, I know about the window, but that was last year. Let's ask him to think again. We [4] .... to him about it.
Karen That's what my mom says, too. She says we could review the rules with the principal again, and we should [5] .... to keep them.
Julian And if he says no?
Karen Then we can [6] .... at school, can't we? My brother told me they organized one four years ago when they weren't allowed to play on the new field and it worked.
Julian OK, let's do that.

2 Answer the questions.

1 What is the problem with the prom?

....

2 What happened last year?

....

3 What did the principal want the students to do?

....

4 What suggestion does Julian make?

....

5 What does Karen's mom suggest?

....

6 What are they planning to do if the principal says no?

....

Language Focus

Vocabulary The environment

1 Complete the sentences with the words below.

distances   plastic bags   recycle   locally produced   litter bugs   save

1 It is very important to .... water.
2 You should really buy .... food.
3 I never use .... at the grocery store.
4 We always .... our glass bottles.
5 Only .... leave bottles and cans on the beach.
6 People shouldn't drive short .... They should ride their bike or walk.

2 Look at the pictures and write what they *should* or *shouldn't* do, using the words in Exercise 1.

1 *She should* ....

2 ....

3 ....

4 ....

5 ....

6 ....

Talking about how green people are

3 Complete the dialogues.

1 **A** Do you sometimes buy locally produced food?
B ....
A Why not?
B ....

2 **A** Do you usually recycle bottles?
B ....
A Where do you take them?
B ....

3 **A** Do you always bring your own bag when you go to the store?
B ....
A Why not?
B ....

Grammar

Reported speech (1)

1 Circle the correct option.

1 She *says / tells* me you aren't coming to the party.
2 You always *say / tell* her that you like her clothes.
3 Tamara *said / told* she's not feeling well.
4 Her parents *said / told* her she can't go out tonight.
5 Sandra *says / tells* him she's angry.
6 We often *tell / say* him that he must try harder.

2 Change the underlined subject pronouns and complete the reported speech sentences.

1 Tony says that .... hungry.

2 Julie says that.......................... good at skiing.

3 Tom says that .... Eminem's latest CD.

4 Harry and Fred say that .... home now.

5 Daisy says that .... the bus.

6 Jessica says that .... him.

want / ask / tell someone to do something

3 **Complete the sentences with the words below.**

not to talk | to tell | ~~to hold~~ | to be | to slow | to buy | not to touch | to take

1 I want you *to hold* my hand.
2 I told you .... careful.
3 I want you .... down. You are driving too fast.
4 I asked you .... it. Now it's broken!
5 I told you .... to her. She'll tell everyone!
6 I asked him .... me a diamond ring.
7 I told you .... a bath.
8 I don't want you .... anyone.

4 **Put the words in parentheses in the correct order.**

1 She (to him get told) some milk on the way home.
She told him to get some milk on the way home.
2 He (her asked to marry) him.
....
3 They (want me didn't leave to).
....
4 We (be him not told to) late.
....
5 She (give me wanted to) her a watch.
....
6 They (us talk to not asked) so loudly.
....
7 I (him drive not asked to) so fast.
....
8 She (told me to call her not) later.
....

5 **Complete the sentences below about yourself.**

1 My mom and dad want me to ....
....
2 My teacher wants me to ....
....
3 I asked my friend not to ....
.... yesterday.
4 My friends wanted me to ....
.... yesterday.

Grammar

6 **Read the dialogue and complete the missing questions.**

Jack I bumped into Dan over the weekend.
Dan *Where did you bump into him?*
Jack At the grocery store.
Dan 1...?
Jack He's doing really well.
Dan 2...?
Jack He's working for a big computer company. He's making a lot of money.
Dan 3.. , wasn't he?
Jack No. We went to the same school, but he wasn't in my class.
Dan 4...?
Jack Yeah, he asked me to go to the theater with him this weekend.
Dan 5...?
Jack I said yes, so we're meeting on Friday.

Sounds right /ɑ/

31 **7** **Listen and repeat.**

1 Don't argue with me.
2 A famous architect designed it.
3 Ask your father.
4 Let's go to the market.
5 An artist carved that sculpture.
6 They marched through the park.

Skills

Listening

32 **1** **Listen to a radio show about a project on women's suffrage. Answer the questions.**

1 What does "suffrage" mean?
2 What did the students and their teacher research first?
3 What did they find out about women's suffrage in
 • the U.S.?
 • Great Britain?
 • Switzerland?
 • Kuwait?
4 Why did they like the project?
5 What is their next project about?

Did you know... ?

In the early 20th century, women in the United States, Great Britain, and Australia demanded the right to vote. These women were called "suffragettes," and they had their own weekly newspaper, *The Suffragette*.

Reading

2 **Read the two newspaper articles and answer the questions.**

The Daily News

March 18, 1912

Christabel Pankhurst flees to Paris!

Christabel Pankhurst, daughter of well-known suffragette Emmeline Pankhurst, has flown to Paris to escape arrest for setting fire to mailboxes, smashing windows, and attacking works of art.

Christabel "Queen of the Mob" Pankhurst is one of the most radical suffragettes. This is not surprising with a family like hers. Her father is a radical lawyer and her mother spends more time in prison than out of it. The Pankhurst women enjoy going on hunger strike for their so-called rights. Maybe they should try cooking a good meal instead!

It is good that the police are now allowed to use the new long-lens cameras. Now they will be able to prove who is behind all the acts of vandalism in our city.

The Suffragette

June 9, 1913

The death of a suffragette

Our friend Emily died yesterday!

1872 - 1913

As our readers all know, Emily threw herself in front of the king's horse Anmer at the Epsom Derby five days ago. She seemed a little better yesterday morning, but her head injuries were terrible, and she died without waking up. Emily Davison gave her life to make the whole world understand that women are serious about the vote.

Emily went to prison three times in 1909 in her fight for women's rights. In the following years she went to prison again and again, she went on hunger strikes, and she was one of the women who started setting fire to mailboxes. She believed that you have to be radical when fighting for your rights. And she believed only something as radical as what she did on June 4 could help our movement.

Emily, we will never forget you!

1 Who was Christabel Pankhurst and why did she flee to Paris?
2 What does the writer say about Christabel's family?
3 What does the writer think about the new long-lens cameras the police have?
4 Who was Emily Davison and why did she die?
5 What kind of protest actions did Emily take part in? What beliefs did she have about them?
6 What is the main difference between the writers of the two articles?

Writing

3 **Read the articles in Exercise 2 and your answers in Exercise 1 again. Write an article about the suffragettes for a magazine. Keep to the following structure.**

Paragraph 1: Explain who the suffragettes were.

Paragraph 2: Use the story of Emmeline Pankhurst as an example of the kinds of actions that the suffragettes took.

Paragraph 3: Say what you think about the suffragettes. Do you think that women have the same rights as men in your country?

California

33 1 **Take the quiz. Then listen and check your answers.**

How much do you know about California?

1

How many people live in California?

a about 15 million c about 35 million
b about 25 million

2

Which city is the state capital of California?

a Los Angeles c San Francisco
b Sacramento

3

Which Californian city has the greatest number of Chinese people outside China?

a Los Angeles c San Francisco
b San Diego

4

What second language do many people in Los Angeles speak?

a Spanish b Italian c Portuguese

5

In which part of Los Angeles do many famous movie stars live?

a Beverly Hills c San Jose
b Anaheim

6

From 1868 to 1963, the island of Alcatraz was a ...

a castle b hotel c prison

7

In 1849, about 40,000 people went to California to look for...

a silver b gold c diamonds

8

One day in 1913, the temperature in Death Valley was...

a 47°C b 57°C c 67°C

9

The Napa Valley is famous for ...

a grapes b oranges c cactuses

10

This Californian group was very famous in the 1960s.

a The Beatles c The Beach Boys
b The Monkees

Language Focus

Vocabulary Physical appearance

1. **Write the words in the correct box.**

casual, sporty, red
blonde, dyed, muscular
thin, dressy, straight
tall, curly, shabby
dirty, short
brown, elegant
black, gray

hair	body	clothes

Identifying a person

2. **You are at a party. You overhear Laura asking about four girls. Write the girls' names below their pictures.**

Laura Who is Alice?
Holly She's the shabby one.
Laura The one with curly blonde hair?
Holly No, the one with straight blonde hair.
Laura OK. And who is Nicole?
Holly She's the one in the skirt with long black hair.
Laura The short one?
Holly No, she's not short.
Laura And who is Leah?
Holly She has long curly hair, and she's wearing jeans and a sweater.
Laura The tall girl?
Holly Yes, that's her. Anybody else?
Laura Yes. Who's Molly?
Holly She's the short, blonde one in torn jeans.
Laura OK. Thanks Holly.

Grammar

Reported speech (2)

1 Circle the correct option.

1 She says that she *is* / *was* going to the party.
2 He said that he *doesn't* / *didn't* like the movie.
3 Dave tells me that you *are* / *were* French.
4 Jeff says that he *wants* / *wanted* some more ice cream.
5 She tells me that he *is* / *was* living in Los Angeles.
6 I told him that I *don't* / *didn't* know her phone number.

2 Write the words that these people said.

1 Jane said she was tired. "I'm tired."
2 Lance said he was going to Hawaii on vacation. ....
3 Paul told me he played soccer on his school team. ....
4 Jack told me he didn't want to come to my party. ....
5 Sharon told me she liked Richard. ....
6 Mr. Bowen said he knew my brother. ....
7 Kerry said she wasn't interested in my story. ....
8 Sam told me my joke was very funny. ....

3 Report what these people are saying.

I'm not afraid of spiders.

1 *She said that she wasn't afraid of spiders.*

I don't like flowers.

2 She told me ....

I'm not from here.

3 The man told us ....

You remind me of someone.

4 She said..........

We want to go home.

5 They said ....

You have beautiful teeth.

6 I told her ....

I'm sorry. I don't have a watch.

7 She said ....

I'm going to bed.

8 He told me ....

4 Match the sentences with the pictures.

1 She asked me if I wanted something to drink.
2 They wanted to know where I was from.
3 He wanted to know when the movie started.
4 The teacher asked him where his homework was.

5 Circle the correct option.

1 He wanted to know if *she was* / *was she* hungry. ....
2 Ben asked me when *did the party start* / *the party started.* ....
3 Dave asked us why *we were* / *were we* angry. ....
4 Penny wanted to know what *my name was* / *was my name.* ....
5 Steve asked Abigail if she *did want* / *wanted* to marry him. ....
6 The teacher asked them why *they were* / *were they* late. ....

6 Put the words in order to make reported sentences.

1 happy / asked / if / I / me / he / was ....
2 she / asked / they / was / if / Chinese / her ....
3 asked / I / me / lived / she / where ....
4 him / asked / I / party / the / started / when ....

7 Tom had a job interview this morning. Report the questions the interviewer asked him.

1 "What's your name?" *She asked Tom what his name was.*
2 "What hobbies do you have?"
....
3 "Why do you want to work for us?"
....
4 "Are you a creative person?"
....
5 "Where do you live?"
....
6 "Do you like sports?"
....
7 "How much do you want to earn?"
....
8 "Do you want to start today?"
....

Skills

Listening

34 **1** **Jake's family went on vacation to California. They rented a car and drove around. They started in San Francisco. Listen and draw their route.**

35 **2** **Listen and find out where Jake saw these things. Write a place name from the map under each photograph.**

1 ....

2 ....

3 ....

4 ....

5 *San Francisco*

6 ....

Reading

3 **Match the words with the definitions. Then read Christine's letter about a dramatic situation in Death Valley.**

1 headquarters a deep valley with steep sides of rock
2 dirt road b road made of hard earth
3 ridge c area at the top of a mountain
4 canyon d main buildings or offices

Did you know...?

Death Valley is about 320 kilometers northeast of Los Angeles. The valley gets less than five centimeters of rain a year and is very hot in the summer months.

3325 Maple Street
Cleveland
4/15/10

Dear Annie,
I have just come back from my vacation in California. I must tell you what happened to me!

The first week of our vacation was great. But then we went to Las Vegas because Oliver wanted to take photos in the mountains around Death Valley.

The first day was fantastic. On the second day we drove our four-wheel drive up into the mountains. We wanted to drive up a canyon. At first, there was a dirt road, but then there were just tracks and after a while we couldn't drive any farther. We got out of the car, took our water bottles and started walking. Soon we were on top of a ridge. We had a wonderful view and Oliver took a lot of photos. But it was very hot and we drank most of the water.

When we wanted to go back, we suddenly couldn't see our car any more! We ran down into the canyon, but the car wasn't there! We were in the wrong canyon! And there was another problem: We had very little water left, and our cell phones didn't work so we couldn't call for help!

Oliver decided to go down into the valley to get help. He wanted me to stay in the shade of a giant rock. Soon I got very thirsty and started to have a terrible headache.

It took Oliver four hours to reach the road. There, a family in a car saw him and took him to the park headquarters. He told them where I was waiting. An hour later a helicopter arrived and took me to a hospital in Las Vegas!

Now I'm back home, and I'm happy that I'm OK again. Hope you had a better vacation than I did! Please write soon!

Your friend, Christine

4 **Answer the questions.**

1 What kind of car did Oliver and Christine rent?
2 Where did Oliver want to take photos?
3 Why did they get out of their car?
4 What did Oliver do when they found out that they were in the wrong canyon?
5 How was Christine rescued?

Writing

5 **Write an answer to Christine's letter, telling her about your last vacation.**

Wordlist

Unit 7

album /'ælbəm/
bamboo /bæm'bu/
binding /'baɪndɪŋ/
blues /bluz/
career /kə'rɪr/
clarinet /ˌklɛrə'nɛt/
classical /'klæsɪkəl/
compilation /ˌkampɪ'leɪʃn/
complaint /kəm'pleɪnt/
country /'kʌntri/
crazy /'kreɪzi/
drummer /'drʌmər/
folk /foʊk/
heavy metal /ˌhɛvi 'mɛtəl/
hip-hop /'hɪp ˌhap/
idol /'aɪdəl/
indie /'ɪndi/
jazz /dʒæz/
lonely /'loʊnli/
to be made up of /bi 'meɪd ˌʌp əv/
massive /'mæsɪv/
metallic /mə'tælɪk/
musician /myu'zɪʃən/
neighbor /'neɪbər/
neither /'niðər/
noise /nɔɪz/
opening /'oʊpənɪŋ/
out of tune /ˌaʊt əv 'tyun/
punk /pʌŋk/
rap /ræp/
to remind /rɪ'maɪnd/
roof /ruf/
to scream /skrim/
to shoot /ʃut/
so /soʊ/
stage /steɪdʒ/
stuff /stʌf/
talent show /'tælənt ˌʃoʊ/
training /'treɪnɪŋ/
vocals /'voʊkəlz/

Unit 8

to affect /æ'fɛkt/
aftershock /'æftərˌʃak/
to amuse /ə'myuz/
artist /'artɪst/
ashore /ə'ʃɔr/
avalanche /'ævəˌlænʃ/
berry /'bɛri/
caption /'kæpʃən/
castaway /'kæstəweɪ/
catastrophe /kə'tæstrəfi/
coconut /'koʊkəˌnʌt/
to collapse /kə'læps/
comic /'kamɪk/
to control /kən'troʊl/
to crush /krʌʃ/
desert island /ˌdɛzərt 'aɪlənd/
disaster /dɪ'zæstər/
dishwasher /'dɪʃˌwɔʃər/
drought /draʊt/
dynamite /'daɪnəˌmaɪt/
earth /ərθ/
earthquake /'ərθˌkweɪk/
to erupt /ɪ'rʌpt/
to escape /ɪs'keɪp/
to evacuate /ɪ'vækyəˌweɪt/
fox /faks/
hurricane /'hərəˌkeɪn/
lava /'lavə/
lightbulb /'laɪtˌbʌlb/
literature /'lɪtərəˌtʃur/
local /'loʊkəl/
make-believe /'meɪk bəˌliv/
miracle /'mɪrɪkəl/
mudslide /'mʌdslaɪd/
nuclear reactor /ˌnukliər ri'æktər/
package /'pækɪdʒ/
to panic /'pænɪk/
peers /pɪrz/
to protect /prə'tɛkt/
raft /ræft/
to reach /ritʃ/
to run into /rʌn 'ɪntə/
to rush /rʌʃ/
scale /skeɪl/
to serve /sərv/
to shake /ʃeɪk/
signal flare /'sɪgnəl flɛr/
to slide /'slaɪd/
society /sə'saɪəti/
strength /strɛŋ(k)θ/
suitcase /'sutˌkeɪs/
survival /sər'vaɪvəl/
to survive /sər'vaɪv/
sympathy /'sɪmpəθi/
telephone /'tɛləˌfoʊn/
temple /'tɛmpəl/
tremor /'trɛmər/
tsunami /(t)su'nami/
volcano /val'keɪnoʊ/
warning /'wɔrnɪŋ/
website /'wɛbsaɪt/
windshield wipers /'wɪn(d)ʃild ˌwaɪpərz/

Unit 9

to add /'æd/
alibi /'æləˌbaɪ/
to babysit /'beɪbiˌsɪt/
bill /bɪl/
bowl /boʊl/
built-in /ˌbɪlt 'ɪn/
to charge /'tʃardʒ/
CD-ROM /ˌsi ˌdi 'ram/
circular /'sərkyələr/
clockwise /'klakwaɪz/
coach /koʊtʃ/
definitely /'dɛfənɪtli/
diagonal /daɪ'ægənəl/
digit /'dɪdʒət/
dilemma /də'lɛmə/
doubt /daʊt/
to earn /ərn/
flash drive /'flæʃ ˌdraiv/
to fold /foʊld/
grade /greɪd/
half /hæf/
horizontal /ˌhɔrə'zantəl/
key /ki/
keyboard /'kiˌbɔrd/
LAN /læn/
to lead to /'lid tə/
modem /'moʊdəm/
to multiply /'mʌltəˌplaɪ/
notebook /'noʊtˌbʊk/
opinion /ə'pɪnyən/
paper route /'peɪpər ˌraʊt/
printer /'prɪntər/
relationship /rɪ'leɪʃənˌʃɪp/
repair /rɪ'pɛr/
ridiculous /rə'dɪkyələs/
to seal /sil/
speakers /'spikərz/
specialist /'spɛʃ(ə)lɪst/
to subtract /səb'trækt/
total /'toʊtəl/

Unit 10

balcony /'bælkəni/
to book /bʊk/
to buy /baɪ/
camping /kæmpɪŋ/
to change /tʃeɪ/
to check out /ˌtʃɛk aʊt/
delta /'dɛltə/
den /dɛn/
to dye /daɪ/
equipment /ɪ'kwɪpmənt/
to find out /ˌfaɪnd 'aʊt/
flight /flaɪt/
ink /ɪŋk/
leopard /'lɛpərd/
to look at /'lʊk ət/
to make /meɪk/
must /mʌs(t)/
opportunity /ˌapər'tunəti/
to paint /peɪnt/
park ranger /ˌpark 'reɪndʒər/
to plot /'plat/
to rent /rɛnt/
safari /sə'fari/
skill /skɪl/
spot /spat/
surfing /'sərfɪŋ/
to take /teɪk/
vacation /veɪkeɪʃən/
volunteer /ˌvalən'tɪə(r)/
wetland /'wɛtˌlænd/
wilderness /'wɪldərnəs/
windsurfing /'wɪndsərfɪŋ/

Unit 11

to admire /əd'maɪ(ə)r/
alternative /ɔl'tərnətɪv/
appliance /ə'plaɪən(t)s/
average /'æv(ə)rɪdʒ/
blackout /'blækaʊt/
blank /blæŋk/
bottle /'batəl/
consumption /kən'sʌm(p)ʃən/
container /kən'teɪnər/
council /'kaʊn(t)səl/
current /'kərənt/
democracy /dɪ'makrəsi/
ecology /ɪ'kalədʒi/
economy /ɪ'kanəmi/
energy /'ɛnərdʒi/
entrance /'ɛntrən(t)s/
to face /feɪs/
to found /faʊnd/
French fries /ˌfrɛntʃ 'fraɪz/
gas pump /'gæs ˌpʌmp/
heat /hit/
hero /'hɪroʊ/
heroine /'hɛrəwən/
increase /ɪŋ'kris/
insulation /ˌɪn(t)sə'leɪʃən/
law /lɔ/
lawyer /'lɔyər/
leaflet /'liflət/

litterbug /ˈlɪtərˌbʌg/
march /mɑrʧ/
marine /məˈrin/
to marry /ˈmɛri/
to object /əbˈʤɛkt/
to overcome /oʊvərˈkʌm/
parliament /ˈpɑrləmənt/
petition /pəˈtɪʃən/
planner /ˈplænər/
plan of action /ˌplæn əv ˈækʃən/
to plant /ˈplɑnt/
playing field /ˈpleɪɪŋ ˌfild/
poison /ˈpɔɪzən/
pond /pɑnd/
to power /ˈpaʊ(ə)r/
protest /ˈproʊtɛst/
to recycle /ˌriˈsaɪkəl/
renewable energy /rɪˌnuəbəl ˈɛnərʤi/
rights /raɪts/
single mother /ˌsɪŋgəl ˈmʌðər/
slogan /ˈsloʊgən/
solar power /ˌsoʊlər ˈpaʊ(ə)r/
source /sɔrs/
to stand up for /ˌstænd ˈʌp fər/
to support /səˈpɔrt/
tennis court /ˈtɛnəs ˌkɔrt/
tide /taɪd/
traditional /trəˈdɪʃnəl/
tunnel /ˈtʌnəl/
washing machine /ˈwɔʃɪŋ məˌʃin/
wind turbine /ˈwɪnd ˌtərbən/

Unit 12

to afford /əˈfɔrd/
blonde /blɑnd/
casual /ˈkæʒwəl/
charts /ʧɑrts/
contrast /ˈkɑntrɑst/
copper /ˈkɑpər/
deal /dil/
diverse /daɪˈvərs/
elegant /ˈɛlɪgənt/
to experience /ɪkˈspɪriən(t)s/
film studio /ˈfɪlm ˌstudioʊ/
generation /ˌʤɛnəˈreɪʃən/
to hand out /ˌhænd ˈaʊt/
handprint /ˈhændprɪnt/
handset /ˈhæn(d)sɛt/
to identify /aɪˈdɛntəˌfaɪ/
incredible /ɪnˈkrɛdəbəl/
influential /ˌɪnfluˈɛn(t)ʃəl/
landfill /ˈlændˌfɪl/
material /məˈtɪriəl/
muscular /ˈmʌskyələr/
national park /ˌnæʃnəl ˈpɑrk/
pipe /paɪp/
politician /ˌpɑləˈtɪʃən/
to release /rɪˈlis/
to reuse /ˌriˈyuz/
scheme /skim/
sophisticated /səˈfɪstəˌkeɪtəd/
sporty /ˈspɔrti/
strip /strɪp/
traffic cone /ˈtræfɪk ˌkoʊn/
up-and-coming /ˌʌp ən(d) ˈkʌmɪŋ/
waste /weɪst/

Pronunciation guide

Vowels

/i/	real, screen
/ɪ/	dish, sit
/ɛ/	chess, bed
/æ/	bad, taxi
/ʌ/	must, done
/ʊ/	good, full
/u/	choose, view
/ə/	dramatic, the
/ɑ/	stop, opera
/ɔ/	saw, daughter

Vowels + /r/

/ər/	first, shirt
/ɑr/	car
/ɔr/	horse
/ɛr/	their
/ʊr/	tourist
/ɪr/	ear

Diphthongs

/eɪ/	play, train
/aɪ/	ice, night
/ɔɪ/	employer, noisy
/aʊ/	house, download
/oʊ/	no, window

Consonants

/p/	push
/b/	bank
/t/	time
/d/	diary
/k/	carpet
/g/	big
/f/	surf
/v/	very
/θ/	thin
/ð/	that
/s/	sit
/z/	zero
/ʃ/	shine
/ʒ/	measure
/h/	hot
/w/	water
/ʧ/	chair
/ʤ/	joke
/m/	more
/n/	snow
/ŋ/	sing
/r/	ring
/l/	small
/y/	you

Grammar Review

Used to — Unit 7

Used to (*didn't use to*) expresses a past routine:
*We **used to** live in town.*
*We **didn't use to** watch TV, but now we watch it every evening.*

The interrogative form *did ... use to?* is rarely used.

So do I / Neither do I — Unit 7

To express agreement we can use the constructions **So** (**do**) **I** answering an affirmative sentence and **Neither** (**do**) **I** answering a negative sentence.
Study the following sentences carefully:
*I like jazz. **So do I**.*
*She can speak English. **So can he**.*
*He went home yesterday**. So did she**.*
*I've never been to the U.S. **Neither have I.***
*We didn't like the party. **Neither did we**.*

too / not enough — Unit 8

Too + adjective means "excessively:"
*It's **too** expensive.*

Not + adjective + **enough** means "not sufficiently:"
*He's **not old enough** to retire.*

Second conditional — Unit 9

The *second conditional* (or *type 2*) consists (like type 1) of an **if-clause** + **main clause.** It is used when we don't expect the action to take place: It has the following structure:

if-clause	**main clause**
if + subject + simple past	*subject + would / wouldn't + infinitive*
***If I had** a lot of money*	***I would buy** a beautiful house*

The meaning does not change if the *main clause* comes before the *if-clause,* but the comma between the two clauses is omitted:
I would buy a beautiful house if I had a lot of money.

The verb in the *if-clause* is in the *simple past.* With the *simple past* of **be** we can use **were** instead of **was** in the first and in the third person singular. The verb in the *main clause* is in the *conditional*:
*If I **were** you, I wouldn't go there.*

Indefinite pronouns — Unit 9

The *indefinite pronouns* are:
someone / somebody; anyone / anybody; no one / nobody; everyone / everybody.

The *indefinite pronouns* follow the same rules as **some** and **any**: the compounds with *some* are used in affirmative sentences; the compounds with *any* are used in negative or interrogative sentences; the compound with *no* = *not* + *any*.

There is no difference in meaning between the compounds with **one** and the compounds with **body**.

Study the following sentences carefully:
Somebody (someone) *called yesterday.*
Has ***anyone (anybody)*** *called?*
I haven't seen ***anybody (anyone)*** or *I've seen* ***nobody (no one).***
Everybody (everyone) *was at the party.*

Causative *have* — Unit 10

Read the following sentences:
I have had my car repaired.
Have you had your hair dyed?

Causative have has the following structure:
have + **object** + **past participle.**

We use *causative have* to say that we have somebody else do something for us.
It can be considered a passive construction.

Infinitive of purpose — Unit 10

Read the following sentences:
I've come ***to help*** *you.*
They called ***to invite*** *us.*
In sentences of this type, the infinitive is used to express purpose.

Reported speech — Units 11 & 12

Reported speech is a construction used to relate someone's opinion, message, or statement, without necessarily using the speaker's exact words. *Reported speech* is usually introduced by the verbs *say* and *tell*. *Say* can be followed by *that* but not by an object pronoun.
He ***says (that)*** *he is hungry.*
Tell can be followed by *that* and is usually followed by an object pronoun.
He ***tells me (that)*** *he is hungry.*
When the reported speech is introduced by *say* or *tell* in the *present* tense there are no changes: the tenses are the same as in the direct speech:
"I am going on vacation." He ***says (tells me)*** *that he's going on vacation.*
"I went to Japan last year." He ***says (tells me)*** *that he went to Japan last year.*

"We will leave tomorrow." They ***say (tell me)*** *they will leave tomorrow.*
Some subject pronouns in direct speech change as follows in reported speech:
I › he / she
you › I
you (plural) **› we**
we › they

If the reported speech is introduced by *say* or *tell* in the *past*, tenses change as follows:

Simple present › Simple past
"I like going shopping." = She said that she liked going shopping.
Present continuous › Past continuous
"We are going home." = They told us that they were going home.
Simple past › Past perfect
"You spoke to the teacher." = He said that I had spoken to the teacher.
Present perfect › Past perfect
"We have been to Japan." = They told me that they had been to Japan.
Will › Would
"I will come as soon as possible." = He said that he would come as soon as possible.

When we report a question, verbs such as *ask* and *wonder* are often used.
Tense changes are the same as for affirmative sentences.
"Are you going home?" He ***asked*** *me if I was going home.*
"Can she speak English?" He ***wondered*** *if she could speak English.*
"Will you come to see us?" They ***asked*** *us if we would come to see them.*

want / ask / tell someone to do something — Unit 11

Want is not followed by a sentence introduced by *that* but has the following structure:

subject	**+ verb**	**+ object**	**+ infinitive**
I	want	him	to come.

Study the following sentence with the negative of the infinitive:
I want you ***not to tell*** *anyone.*

Verbs such as **love, like, prefer,** and **wish** have the same structure as **want.**

Instruções de uso do CD-ROM

Instalação

Insira o CD-ROM **American MORE!** no compartimento de CD e siga na tela as instruções de instalação.
Se as instruções não aparecerem na tela, entre em *Meu Computador*, clique em D (ou no *drive* apropriado). Em seguida dê um duplo-clique no ícone *American More!* para iniciar a instalação.
Para usar o CD-ROM, dê um duplo-clique no atalho **American MORE!** criado na área de trabalho.

Conteúdo do CD-ROM

Exercícios interativos complementares para prática de vocabulário, gramática, pronúncia, leitura, compreensão oral e produção escrita, além de jogos divertidos. Clique em uma das unidades (Starter-12) e selecione uma das atividades para começar.

Configurações de sistema recomendadas

Windows 2000/XP/: 256MB RAM (mín. 512 MB)
Windows Vista/7: 1GB RAM (mín. 2GB)

Suporte

Para resolver problemas técnicos relacionados ao uso deste CD-ROM, acesse: www.cambridge.org/elt/multimedia/help

Termos e condições de uso para o **American MORE!** CD-ROM

1 Licença

(a) A Cambridge University Press e a Editora Ática concedem licença de uso desse CD-ROM (i) em um único computador para uma ou mais pessoas em momentos diferentes, ou (ii) para uma única pessoa em um ou mais computadores (contanto que o CD-ROM seja usado somente em um computador por vez e por apenas um usuário).

(b) Em relação ao conteúdo desse CD-ROM, o usuário não poderá: (i) copiar ou autorizar a cópia, (ii) traduzir, (iii) inverter a ordem ou alterar a estrutura, (iv) transferir, vender, delegar ou ceder qualquer parte, ou (v) disponibilizar em uma rede ou servidor.

2 Direitos Autorais

Todo conteúdo do CD-ROM é protegido pela lei de direito autoral e propriedade intelectual. O usuário adquire apenas o direito de uso do CD-ROM sem qualquer outro direito sobre seu conteúdo, expresso ou oculto, que não aqueles expressos na licença.

3 Obrigações

No âmbito jurídico, a Cambridge University Press e a Editora Ática não se responsabilizam por danos ou perdas de qualquer natureza decorrentes do uso desse produto ou de quaisquer erros e problemas no CD-ROM. Em todos os casos as obrigações das editoras se limitam ao valor real pago pelo produto.

Workbook 3 – Audio CD

Track	Time	Track	Time	Track	Time	Track	Time
1.	0'44"	10.	1'36"	19.	0'31"	28.	0'34"
2.	1'05"	11.	0'50"	20.	1'25"	29.	2'11"
3.	0'49"	12.	2'05"	21.	0'33"	30.	1'17"
4.	1'11"	13.	1'22"	22.	3'02"	31.	0'44"
5.	1'58"	14.	1'21"	23.	3'02"	32.	2'44"
6.	0'46"	15.	1'38"	24.	1'06"	33.	1'45"
7.	3'11"	16.	1'15"	25.	0'46"	34.	1'24"
8.	0'58"	17.	0'47"	26.	0'41"	35.	2'04"
9.	1'35"	18.	0'45"	27.	3'01"		

Total Duration: 50min46s